CityPack
Los Angeles

EMMA STANFORD

Emma Stanford's first visit to LA was as a teenager: she discovered Disneyland and Gap Teens. Since then her LALAland explorations (both touristic and sartorial) have clocked up many thousands of freeway miles, several wild spending sprees and an insider knowledge to rival most Angelenos. She loves her sea and sun and has written AA Explorer Hawaii *and* Explorer Florida.

City-centre map continues on inside back cover

AA Publishing

Contents

About this book

KEY TO SYMBOLS

✚ map reference on the fold-out map accompanying this book (see below)

⊠ address

☎ telephone number

🕐 opening times

🍴 restaurant or café on premises or nearby

🚇 nearest Metro (underground) train station

🚃 nearest overground train station

🚌 nearest bus route

⛴ nearest riverboat or ferry stop

♿ facilities for visitors with disabilities

✋ admission charge

↔ other nearby places of interest

❓ tours, lectures, or special events

► indicates the page where you will find a fuller description

ℹ tourist infomation

CityPack Los Angeles is divided into six sections to cover the six most important aspects of your visit to Los Angeles. It includes:

- The author's view of the city and its people
- Itineraries, walks and excursions
- The top 25 sights to visit – as selected by the author
- Features about different aspects of the city that make it special
- Detailed listings of restaurants, hotels, shops and nightlife
- Practical information

In addition, easy-to-read side panels provide fascinating extra facts and snippets, highlights of places to visit and invaluable practical advice.

CROSS-REFERENCES

To help you make the most of your visit, cross-references, indicated by ►, show you where to find additional information about a place or subject.

MAPS

- **The fold-out map** in the wallet at the back of the book is a comprehensive street plan of Los Angeles. All the map references given in the book refer to this map. For example, the Natural History Museum, 900 Exposition Boulevard has the following information: ✚ J11 indicating the grid square of the map in which the Natural History Museum will be found.

- **The city-centre maps** found on the inside front and back covers of the book itself are for quick reference. They show the Top 25 Sights, described on pages 24–48, which are clearly plotted by number (**❶** – **㉕**, not page number) from west to east.

PRICES

Where appropriate, an indication of the cost of an establishment is given by **£** signs: **£££** denotes higher prices, **££** denotes average prices, while **£** denotes lower charges.

LOS ANGELES
life

A PERSONAL VIEW

Driving

The best way to get around LA is by car. And that means braving the freeways. In truth, this is not as scary as it may seem. However, plan your journey in advance, leave plenty of time, and avoid rush hour periods and 'car pool' lanes unless you have the requisite number of passengers. Angelenos often refer to freeways by name, not number, they drive fast, change lanes more often than their socks, and cultivate a complete disregard for other traffic sharing the road.

Mural at Venice Beach

Welcome to LALALand! A land of sunshine, promise and wealth beyond the dreams of avarice. Squeezed into a 1,000-square-mile basin encircled by picturesque mountains and the Pacific Ocean, this vast urban megalopolis is home to movie stars and Mickey Mouse, richly endowed art museums and pneumatic babes. LA (locals never spell out 'Los Angeles') is balanced on the cutting edge of cool, where restaurants, cars, pets and people blister in and out of fashion in the blink of an eye. Tinseltown is also a master of illusion with a pedigree stretching back to the dawn of the Hollywood movie era. Behind the palm trees and the power lunches, earthquakes, mud slides and grinding poverty are all part of the deal, and they lend LA an uncompromising edge far more realistic than the vicariously reported low-life dabblings of the Hollywood set.

That said, few visitors will run into a single member of the Crips or the Bloods (LA's two most notorious streets gangs) even if they go looking. And the statistical likelihood of being caught in a major earthquake is remote. You are more likely to suffer financially from valet parking, a legalised form of daylight robbery in a city landscaped by the combustion engine, where everybody drives everywhere.

Since LA was founded by missionary farmers in 1781, the Downtown area has moved only a couple of blocks from the original site. Bounded by freeways, it remains the hub of the city, a highrise corporate ghetto where all eyes are focused on the burgeoning Pacific Rim markets over the horizon. Beyond Downtown is Los Angeles County, made up of 88 incorporated cities and dozens of individual neighbourhoods. On paper, it looks like a cultural melting pot

Downtown Los Angeles, backed by the San Gabriel Mountains

combining the largest Hispanic and Asian/Pacific populations, and fourth largest black population in the US. In reality, the neighbourhoods are deeply segregated along racial lines, and tensions are never far below the surface.

Cut a broad swath west of Downtown to the Pacific shore at Santa Monica, and you will find the majority of the city's top sightseeing attractions, shopping, dining and entertainment opportunities. Hollywood, West Hollywood, Beverly Hills and West LA are the fickle heart of LALALand, where star-struck celebrities come out at night to watch each other in Spago or Tatou, at Johnny Depp's Viper Room, or at the Improv. Of course, if you go and look for them, they are never there. The only way to ensure celebrity-spotting in Tinseltown is to get a ticket for the *Tonight Show*.

However, if genuine stars are in short supply, there is nothing to prevent you from hamming it up in a dozen familiar-from-the-big (or small) screen locations, from Union Station (*Bladerunner*) to the Griffith Park Observatory (*Rebel Without a Cause*). LA is definitely the place to indulge fantasies. Hire a limo for an evening out, wear sunglasses around the clock, hob-nob with Goofy at Disneyland, and dress up for window shopping in Beverly Hills, then flounce into the Regent Beverly Wilshire (the *Pretty Woman* hotel) for a cocktail.

Literary LA

There is no better place to read Raymond Chandler's dark, gritty crime novels than in the city that inspired them in the 1930s and 1940s. Evelyn Waugh's satirical look at the American way of death, *The Loved One*, is based on LA's Forest Lawn Cemetery; Nathaniel West rips into early Hollywood in *Day of the Locust*; and Hollywood insider Julia Phillips lays bare 'the industry' in modern times with *You'll Never Eat Lunch in this Town Again*.

A Day in the Life of an Angeleno

TGIF

Weekends in LA begin on a Friday night when Westwood Village goes pedestrian to cope with crowds sauntering between sidewalk cafés, cinemas and record stores. Santa Monica's Third Street Promenade is another hot spot. On Sunday mornings, brunch at the beach is an institution in the South Bay area, and no first-time visitor to LA should miss the colourful street parade that is Venice Beach at the weekend.

They say nine out of ten Angelenos would prefer to live in Santa Monica. One of the chief charms of waking up in this oceanfront neighbourhood is, of course, the beach, and in the misty early morning, joggers and power walkers are already out pounding along the beach path.

By 7am, LA's 800 miles of freeway hell are clogging up. The average commuter drives a 30-mile round-trip daily and, with coffee balanced on the dashboard, checks local radio stations for traffic information, weather conditions and (in summer) the all-important smog report.

Angelenos 'do' lunch from before midday to 1 or 2pm. Whether they grab a deli sandwich or graze on a prohibitively expensive salad with designer leaves, mineral water is the typical accompaniment. The freeway mayhem begins again around 4:30pm until 7pm, and by early evening the city's gyms are packed with lycra-clad bodies being honed to perfection.

Showered and refreshed, it might be time for a cocktail before dinner. LA's watering holes run the gamut from unpretentious bars to the rarified atmosphere of the Polo Lounge, a renowned movie mogul haunt in the Beverly Hills Hotel. Shopping malls are busy in the evening, too, as shops stay open until 9 or 10. Westwood Village is a good place to catch dinner and a first-run movie; or join the cultural classes for a concert at Downtown's Music Center. Melrose Avenue has hip eateries and comedy clubs but the poseurs' paradise is a sidewalk table on Sunset Plaza, ready to hit the Sunset Strip music club zone later.

Taking the dog for a walk, Venice Beach style

LOS ANGELES IN FIGURES

DISTANCES
- Distance from San Francisco: 397 miles
- Distance from New York: 2,767 miles
- Distance from London: 5,460 miles
- Distance from San Andreas fault: 33 miles (from Downtown)

AREA/ POPULATION
- City of Los Angeles: 465 square miles/3.4 million people
- Los Angeles Five County Area: 34,149 square miles/14.5 million people
- Number of incorporated cities in the Five County Area: 88

GEOGRAPHY
- Latitude: 34° 04'N
- Longitude: 118° 15'W
- LA is on approximately the same latitude as Atlanta, Casablanca, Beirut, Kashmir and Osaka
- Highest point: Mt Wilson, 5,710 feet
- Lowest point: sea level
- Miles of shoreline in Five County Area: 160 (Los Angeles County: 74)

HISTORY
- Founded: El Pueblo de Nuestra Señora la Reina de Los Angeles, 4 September 1781
- Number of settlers: 44
- Oldest house: Avila Adobe (1818)
- Declared a city: 1836

REVENUE & COMMUNICATIONS
- Annual turnover in Los Angeles Customs district: $146 billion
- Annual movie industry receipts: around $19 billion
- Annual total direct visitor expenditure: $9.25 billion
- Miles of freeway: around 800

WEATHER
- Warmest months: July–August (average 83°/63°F max/min)
- Coolest month: January (average 65°/45°F max/min)
- Wettest month: February
- Smog season: May to October

9

A Chronology

Pre-1781	Indian village of Yang-Na near Los Angeles River, close to present-day site of City Hall. Mission of San Gabriel Archangel founded 1771 in San Gabriel Valley (▶ 12).
1781	*Los Pobladores*, 44 farmer-settlers from the San Gabriel mission establish El Pueblo de Nuestra Señora la Reina de Los Angeles in the fertile Los Angeles basin.
1818	The Avila Adobe house is built for Don Francisco Avila, wealthy cattle rancher and mayor of Los Angeles from 1810.
1825	California becomes a territory of Mexico.
1842	Gold is discovered in the San Fernando Valley, six years before the discovery at Sutter's Mill which triggered the Gold Rush.
1848	End of the Mexican-American War. California becomes part of the United States. (Achieves statehood 1850.)
1872	The Southern Pacific Railroad Company commissions the first guidebook to Southern California. Charles Nordhoff's *California: For Health, Pleasure and Residence* creates a flood of visitors.
1876	The first transcontinental railroad arrives in Los Angeles.
1880	The University of Southern California is founded with 53 students and 12 teachers.
1881	General Harrison Gray Otis publishes the first issue of the *Los Angeles Times*.
1888	The city's first black community is established at First and Los Angeles streets.
1892	Edward Doheny discovers oil in Downtown.
1902	LA's first movie house, the Electric Theatre, opens on Main Street.

1909	Santa Monica Pier opens to attract tourists.
1911	The Nestor Co begins making movies in LA.
1913	Cecil B De Mille makes the first full-length film, *The Squaw Man*.
1915	D W Griffith (▶12) writes, directs and produces his controversial Civil War epic *The Birth of a Nation*.
1919	United Artists Film Corp founded by D W Griffith, Mary Pickford, Douglas Fairbanks and Charlie Chaplin to improve actors' lot.
1927	The Academy of Motion Picture Arts and Sciences is founded at the Biltmore Hotel.
1932	The Olympic Summer Games come to Exposition Park.
1940	Inauguration of LA's first freeway, the Arroyo Seco Parkway.
1955	Disneyland opens.
1964	The Beatles perform at the Hollywood Bowl.
1965	Race riots in Watts, LA's black ghetto, rage for six days leaving 34 dead and 1,032 wounded.
1984	The Olympic Summer Games return to LA.
1990	I M Pei's First Interstate World Center becomes the tallest building west of Chicago.
1992	Riots follow acquittal of four white police officers on charges of beating a black motorist (▶12).
1993	Brush fires threaten Malibu and cause more than $200 million-worth of damage.
1994	Northridge earthquake (6.8 on the Richter scale) kills 55 and does $30 billion damage.

PEOPLE & EVENTS FROM HISTORY

The Los Angeles Aqueduct

As Los Angeles boomed around the turn of the 20th century, the demand for water became a major issue. When water bureau superintendent William Mulholland suggested building an aqueduct to transport melted snow from the Sierra Nevadas to feed the growing city, they thought he was mad. However, Mulholland's aqueduct, all 223 miles and 142 tunnels of it, opened in 1913, and with a 105-mile extension into the Mono Basin, it still supplies 80 per cent of the city's requirements.

FATHER JUNÍPERO SERRA

Born on the Mediterranean island of Mallorca in 1713, Father Junípero was sent to Mexico to work as a missionary in 1749. In 1769, as Padre Presidente of the Spanish Franciscan missions in Baja (Lower) California, he accompanied the first governor of the Californias, Gaspar de Portolá, on a colonising expedition to San Diego. Here they founded the first of 21 California missions in a chain which would reach from San Diego north to Sonoma. San Gabriel Archangel, in the San Gabriel Valley, was the fourth, built with the help of Native Americans, later known as Gabrieleno Indians.

D W GRIFFITH

David Wark Griffith (1875–1948) is often regarded as the greatest pioneer and innovator in the history of film-making. He began his career in New York, then moved to Los Angeles where he made *The Birth of a Nation* (banned in some cities for its racist tone), followed in 1916 by *Intolerance* with Lillian Gish and lavish Babylonian sets. Working with cameraman Billy Bitzer, Griffith experimented with lighting and camera techniques. An early champion of the 'talkies', which he claimed would become 'the greatest artistic medium the world has ever known', Griffith was also responsible for toning down the melodramatic proclivities of contemporary stage actors.

THE 1992 LA RIOTS

When the videotaped 1991 beating of black motorist Rodney King by white LAPD officers failed to secure a single court conviction, racial tensions amongst LA's black community exploded in the country's most destructive episode of civil unrest this century. The first outbreak of violence came within hours of the not-guilty verdicts being delivered on 29 April 1992. Some 48 hours later, 52 people were dead, 2,400 injured, 1,600 businesses were closed for good, and the property damage bill exceeded $1 billion.

D W Griffiths directing Battle of the Sexes

LOS ANGELES
how to organise your time

ITINERARIES

Los Angeles is so vast it makes sense to sightsee by area and a car is almost essential. It is a good idea to check the map in advance and plot a route. With the notable exception of Downtown, parking is easy and inexpensive.

ITINERARY ONE	**HOLLYWOOD BOULEVARD TO HOLLYHOCK HOUSE**
Morning	Start off outside Mann's Chinese Theater (➤ 55), then cross the street to the Hollywood Roosevelt Hotel (➤ 53) for a Hollywood history lesson. Stop by the Museum of Hollywood History (➤ 53), Hollywood Guinness World of Records Museum (➤ 58) and Frederick's of Hollywood Lingerie Museum (➤ 52).
Lunch	Celebrity-spot at Musso & Frank Grill (➤ 64), or picnic in Barnsdall Park at Hollyhock House (➤ 34). Late lunchers will find plenty of options on Melrose Avenue (➤ 70).
Afternoon	After a tour of Hollyhock House, take a detour via the Hollywood Memorial Park Cemetery (➤ 52) to Melrose Avenue (➤ 70).
ITINERARY TWO	**SOUTH BAY (PALOS VERDES TO LONG BEACH)**
Morning	Take the scenic route around the Palos Verdes headland (off the Pacific Coast Highway) via Lloyd Wright's Wayfarer's Chapel to San Pedro and the Los Angeles Maritime Museum (➤ 50). Kids might enjoy the free Cabrillo Marine Aquarium (➤ 59) near by. The Banning Residence Museum (➤ 50) is *en route* to Long Beach and the *Queen Mary* (➤ 42). This is a good place to break for lunch.
Lunch	Belmont Brewing Company (➤ 63); Shenandoah Café (➤ 68); or budget fillers from Tony's Famous French Dip Sandwiches (➤ 63).
Afternoon	The *Queen Mary* is berthed a couple of minutes from Downtown. A 10-minute drive west, Rancho Los Alamitos (➤ 43) is a delight.

| ITINERARY THREE | **PASADENA** |

Morning

The Huntington (►46) deserves a full day in its own right. However, Pasadena has much else to offer starting with the historic Mission San Gabriel Archangel (►56). The Los Angeles State and County Arboretum (►47) is a real treat, and the Descanso Gardens (►57) are famous for camellias (Jan–Mar). Then head for Old Town Pasadena (►70).

Lunch

Colorado Boulevard's Pasadena Baking Company (►63) or nextdoor neighbour Mia Piace are two good options. Also the Gordon Biersch Brewery (►69) and The Raymond (►64).

Afternoon

Two cultural gems to enjoy are the stunning Art and Crafts Movement Gamble House (►44) and the Norton Simon Museum of Art (►45). Both are only open afternoons, Thursday to Sunday.

ITINERARY FOUR   **SANTA MONICA TO VENICE BEACH**

Morning

Shoppers shouldn't miss Third Street Promenade and Santa Monica Place (►70–71). Then head straight for Santa Monica Pier (►24). Hire a bike for the day and coast down the beach bike path with detours off to shops and galleries on Main Street (between Hollister and Rose Avenues), also home to architect Frank Gehry's Edgemar development (2435 Main) and the California Heritage Museum (2612 Main).

Lunch

Try the terrace at Rockenwagner (►65), the patio of the World Café (►68), or Venice's beachfront Sidewalk Café (►68) for excellent people-watching.

Afternoon

If the beach does not beckon after lunch, take a stroll around the canal district (►24); stop by the landmark Chiat/Day Inc Advertising Building (►54); and visit the Museum of Flying (►58).

WALKS

AROUND DOWNTOWN: PERSHING SQUARE TO LITTLE TOKYO

Start off at Pershing Square with its purple bell-tower and multicoloured building block installa-

tions, then cut through the sumptuously refurbished Biltmore Hotel to Grand Avenue. The LA Conservancy's guided walking tours (▶ 19) depart from the Biltmore on Saturday mornings. Take a turn around the Los Angeles Central Library, then climb the Bunker Hill Steps from the foot of the First Interstate World Center opposite.

All aboard Angel's Flight

Bunker Hill At the top of the city's steep, glass-canyoned Financial District, the Wells Fargo History Museum is just across the road from the Museum of Contemporary Art (MOCA) and California Plaza. The Plaza is a good place to catch your breath and watch the dancing fountains before taking the Angel's Flight down to Grand Central Market. Walk through the Market and cross Broadway to the Bradbury Building.

Coffee breaks There are several sidewalk café-coffee shops on the Bunker Hill Steps and at the Wells Fargo Center, plus the up-scale cafeteria Patinette at MOCA, 250 S Grand Avenue (☎ 213/626 1178).

Little Tokyo Shuttle bus DASH D operates from Spring Street to Union Station. If you have time for a detour, it passes within a block of Little Tokyo, or walk to Second Street and then east for Japanese Village Plaza.

Time for lunch Grand Central Market is a great place to eat cheaply; bakers, fruit sellers and deli stalls offer everything from Mexican tacos to Chinese noodles. Near Union Station, there is Philippe The Original (▶ 63), and a number of Mexican restaurants including La Golondrina (▶ 66) on Olvera Street.

THE SIGHTS

- Biltmore Hotel (▶ 56)
- Los Angeles Central Library (▶ 56)
- Wells Fargo History Museum (▶ 36)
- MOCA (▶ 37)
- California Plaza (▶ 54)
- Angel's Flight (▶ 54)
- Grand Central Market (▶ 38)
- Bradbury Building (▶ 39)
- Little Tokyo (▶ 40)

INFORMATION

Time 2–3 hours
Distance approx 1½ miles
Start point Pershing Square
🚇 M7
🚊 Pershing Square
🚌 DASH B, C, E
End point Little Tokyo
🚇 N7
🚌 DASH A, D

AROUND EL PUEBLO: UNION STATION TO CHINATOWN

Take time to explore inside the splendid Spanish Colonial-style Union Station building before walking up to the Old Plaza at the heart of El Pueblo de Los Angeles, the centre of the oldest settlement here. The tree-shaded plaza is flanked by historic buildings including the three-storey, 1870 Pico House built by the last Mexican governor of California.

Olvera Street Stroll down this restored 19th-century street, tightly packed with the souvenir and craft stalls of a Mexican street market wedged between the brick façades. Here lively sidewalk restaurants, and take-away taco stands, ice-cream and *churros* vendors do a swift trade. Stop off at the city's oldest dwelling, the Avila Adobe, founded in 1818 and since then much enlarged, along the way. The Visitor Information Center, located in the Sepulveda House, presents a short video showing a brief history of Los Angeles.

Avila Adobe, the city's oldest abode

Chinatown Walk west a couple of blocks to Broadway, then north. Though no match for San Francisco's bustling Chinatown, the 900 block of Broadway boasts a handful of oriental-inspired bank buildings in the Bank of America, the East-West Bank guarded by stone lion-dogs, and the United Savings Bank on the corner of kitsch Sun-Yat-Sen Plaza. Amongst the restaurants and fortune tellers around the plaza, there is a well-used wishing well and shops selling a wide assortment of wares including incense, jade carvings, pottery and plum sauce.

THE SIGHTS

● Union Station (➤ 56)
● El Pueblo de Los Angeles Historic Park and Olvera Street (➤ 41)

INFORMATION

Time 1½–2 hours
Distance approx 1¼ miles
Start point Union Station
⊞ N6
🚇 Union Station
🚌 DASH B, D
End point Chinatown
⊞ N5
🚌 DASH B

EVENING STROLLS

Although LA is a car town, there are a couple of pedestrian-friendly enclaves where a pre-prandial stroll is in order.

OLD PASADENA

Perfect for a gentle amble combined with a spot of window-shopping (▶70), this three-block section of Colorado Boulevard, in one of LA's most affluent suburbs, also offers a wide choice of restaurants. Admire the handsome old brick buildings ornamented with decorative reliefs and wrought ironwork.

OLVERA STREET

El Pueblo's Mexican street market continues well into the evening. Souvenir-hunting followed by a spot of people-watching with a pre-dinner *margarita* is a favourite pastime here.

SANTA MONICA

Watch the sunset from the pier, then stroll to the pedestrianised Third Street Promenade, which is edged by dozens of bars, cafés, shops and restaurants that open until late.

WESTWOOD VILLAGE

The magic triangle of Westwood Boulevard, Broxton and Weyburn avenues on the southern edge of the UCLA campus was actually designed to be pedestrian-friendly, a rare quality in LA. The architecture is 1920s Mediterranean Revival; sidewalk cafés, coffee bars and restaurants abound; and this is the place to catch first-run movies.

INFORMATION

Old Pasadena
Start point Between Arroyo
    Parkway and Delacey
    Avenue
🚫 Off map, northeast
🚌 180, 181, 484

Olvera Street
Start point Old Plaza, El Pueblo
    de Los Angeles
🚫 N6
🚊 Union Station
🚌 DASH B, D

Santa Monica
Start point Santa Monica Pier
🚫 Off map, west
🚌 22

Westwood Village
Start point Westwood Boulevard
    (off Wilshire)
🚫 Off map, west
🚌 20, 21, 22

The pier at Santa Monica is a favourite filming location

ORGANISED SIGHTSEEING

WALKING TOURS

Los Angeles Conservancy (☎ 213/623 2489) Excellent Saturday morning Downtown walk tours with options ranging from historic Broadway theatres to art deco architecture.

JRT International – 'Hiking in L.A.' (☎ 818/501 1005) Scenic hiking tours in the Santa Monica Mountains.

BUS TOURS

Hollywood Fantasy Tours (☎ 213/469 8184) The classic 'star tours' formula covering the highlights and movie star homes of Hollywood and Beverly Hills.

Oskar J's Sightseeing Tours (☎ 818/501 2217) A wide range of tour options including Hollywood celebrity haunts and houses, helicopter tours and harbour cruises.

LIMOUSINE TOURS

Star Limousine Tours (☎ 310/829 1066) and **Ultra Tours** (☎ 310/274 1303) both offer tours of star homes and Hollywood highlights in stretch-limo luxury.

HELICOPTER TOURS

Heli U.S.A. Helicopters (☎ 310/651 9494) A great romantic night-time package with a spectacular flight over the city lights followed by dinner at DC3 (▶ 69). Also daytime flights.

KF Aviation (☎ 818/557 0997) Top Gun with tunes: swoop over Hollywood and Beverly Hills with Air Opera surround-sound cabin entertainment and peek at the stars around their pools.

BOAT TRIPS

Gondola Getaway (☎ 310/433 9595) BYO champagne and the stripey-shirted gondolier will provide ice bucket, glasses and hors d'oeuvres to accompany a Venetian-style gondola ride around the canals of Naples Island (Long Beach).

Shoreline Village Cruises (☎ 310/495 5884) Summer season harbour cruises and whale-watching expeditions (Jan–Apr) from Long Beach. Guaranteed whale sightings, or second trip for free.

NBC Studio tours

The only LA television studio to offer tours, NBC Studio (above), 3000 W Alameda Avenue, Burbank (☎ 818/840 3537), invites visitors to take a look around its broadcasting complex. Check out the wardrobe and make-up departments, visit a special effects set and *The Tonight Show* set. Free tickets for the evening show are available at the Studio's ticket counter.

Excursions

INFORMATION

J Paul Getty Museum
- Off map, west
- 17985 Pacific Coast Highway
- For parking reservations (1–2 weeks in advance) and information, 310/458 2003
- Tue–Sun 10–5
- 434 from Santa Monica. Ask driver for free admission pass
- Free

Topanga State Park
- Off map, west
- 20825 Entrada Road
- 310/455 2465
- Daily 8–7 in summer; 8–5 in winter
- Moderate parking fee

Solstice Canyon Park
- Off map, west
- 310/456 7154
- 3800 Solstice Canyon Road
- Daily 8–sunset
- Moderate parking fee
- 434 to Corral Canyon Road

J PAUL GETTY MUSEUM, MALIBU

From 1997, the new Getty Center (▶ 25) will house the bulk of the Getty collections, while the Malibu site will become a centre for antiquities. The superb collections of Greek and Roman art are housed in a spectacular reconstruction of a Roman villa based on the Villa dei Papyri destroyed by the eruption of Mount Vesuvius which also engulfed Pompeii in AD 79. There are beautiful gardens to explore, short introductory talks, a picnic site and the Garden Tea Room.

HIKING IN THE SANTA MONICA MOUNTAINS

One mile west of the Getty Museum, Topanga Canyon Boulevard climbs up from the Malibu seashore into the foothills of the Santa Monica Mountains. As it passes through the laidback alternative community of Topanga Canyon, bear right for Topanga State Park. Trails crisscross the 9,000-acre chaparral reserve, winding through oak and sumac woodlands and across rolling pastures with views of the mountains and off to the ocean. Look out for red-tailed hawks wheeling overhead, California quail and even the occasional roadrunner.

Solstice Canyon Park, a former ranch off the Pacific Coast Highway just west of Malibu, is reckoned to have one of the finest walking trails in the mountains. There are two routes which form a convenient loop: the gentle 1½-mile Solstice International Trail, which is shady in summer, along an old ranch road to a waterfall grotto fed by Solstice Creek; and the connecting Rising Sun Trail, a 3-mile high chaparral hike with notable views.

CATALINA ISLAND

Take the Catalina Cruises ferry (1 hour 50 minutes), or the Catalina Express hydrofoil (1 hour 10 minutes) to Avalon, and drop in at the Chamber of Commerce office on the pier for a map, sightseeing, glass-bottomed boat and dive tour information (also hiking permits if required). Explore Avalon, stopping off at the marvellous 1920s Casino and the Catalina Museum, then climb the hill to the Zane Grey Pueblo Hotel (➤ 85) for the harbour view. The Catalina Safari Bus offers cheap scheduled transport to Two Harbours, and to campgrounds and beaches across the miraculously undeveloped island interior. An overnight stay is highly recommended, but accommodation is limited and often booked up well in advance.

SAN JUAN CAPISTRANO

The seventh of the California missions, San Juan Capistrano was founded in 1776. Take time to wander in the pretty gardens, shaded by jacaranda trees and bright in season with camellias, roses, hibiscus, and bougainvillea. There is a blacksmith's shop and restored barrack buildings housing Spanish-era artefacts, plus the lovely painted adobe Serra Chapel. The picturesque ruins of the Stone Church are home to the famous swallows which are said to return here from Argentina for the

San Juan Capistrano

summer every 19 March. Beyond the mission, the town offers a number of Spanish-style buildings and several antiques stores (good for browsing) on Camino Capistrano, plus a local history museum, across the railroad tracks.

The two main driving routes south to this small mission town are the fast, direct I-5/Santa Ana Freeway (about an hour from Downtown to the I-74 exit) and the slower Pacific Coast Highway, passing through Huntington, Newport and Laguna Beaches.

INFORMATION

Catalina

➕ Off map, southwest

☎ For Catalina Cruises (Long Beach) information 1–800/228 2546; Catalina Express (Long Beach and San Pedro) information 1–800/464 4228; Catalina Island Chamber of Commerce and Visitor's Bureau ☎ 310/510 1520

Mission San Juan Capistrano

✉ Camino Capistrano at Ortega Highway

☎ 714/284 2049

🕐 Daily 8:30–5

🚂 Trains from Union Station

💲 Moderate

WHAT'S ON

Angelenos love a festival and the local calendar is overflowing with special events. For up-to-date details of what's on where, check with the Los Angeles Convention and Visitor Bureau Events Hotline (☎213/689 8822). The multi-lingual service lists local happenings across the board from museum exhibitions to sports. The Calendar section of Sunday's *Los Angeles Times* provides a weekly guide to events, as does the widely available freebie, *LA Weekly*.

JANUARY | *Rose Parade*: Pasadena's all-singing, all-dancing New Year's Day spectacular and Rose Bowl football game is televised around the nation

FEBRUARY | *Chinese New Year*: the Golden Dragon Parade winds its way through Chinatown

MARCH | *Academy Awards*: celebrities gather Downtown for an orgy of back-slapping

MAY | *Cinco de Mayo*: Mexican celebrations. Olvera Street is a good place to join in the fun

JUNE | *Gay and Lesbian Pride Celebration*: massive weekend event held around West Hollywood Park. June also marks the start of the California Plaza free lunchtime concert season (Jun–Oct)

JULY | *Hollywood Bowl Summer Festival*: nightly (Jul–Sep) open-air concerts with broad-ranging programme – classical music, jazz and pops

AUGUST | *Nisei Week*: dance and martial arts demonstrations, crafts and food stalls as Little Tokyo celebrates Japanese-American cultural heritage

OCTOBER | *AFI Film Festival*: the American Film Institute descends on LA for a two-week film binge

NOVEMBER | *Dia de los Muertos*: folklorico musicians, puppet shows, Mexican music and crafts on Olvera Street for the Day of the Dead
Doo Dah Parade: Pasadena's irreverent Rose Parade spoof

DECEMBER | Hollywood Christmas Parade: one of the larger Yule-themed events featuring floats, marching bands, classic cars and celebrity guests

LOS ANGELES'
top 25 sights

The sights are shown on the maps on the inside front cover and inside back cover, numbered **1–25** *from west to east across the city*

1

SANTA MONICA & VENICE BEACH

HIGHLIGHTS

- Main Street galleries and restaurants
- Muscle Beach
- Natural Elements Sculpture Park
- Ocean Front Walk
- Pacific Coast Bicentennial Bike Route
- Santa Monica Pier
- Sunset from Palisades Park, on Ocean Avenue, by Santa Monica and Wilshire boulevards
- Third Street Promenade
- Venice Canal Walkway (access from S Venice Boulevard)

INFORMATION

➕ Off map, west
Santa Monica Visitor Center
✉ 1400 Ocean Avenue (between Santa Monica Boulevard and Colorado Avenue)
☎ 310/393 7593
🕐 Daily 10–4 (until 5 in summer)
🚌 4, 20, 22, 33, 304, 320, 333
♿ Good to non-existent depending on location
↔ Bergamot Station (➤ 74), Chiat/Day Inc Advertising Building (➤ 54), J Paul Getty Museum (➤ 20), Museum of Flying (➤ 58), Will Rogers State Historic Park (➤ 57)
❓ Walk tours of Santa Monica murals (☎ 310/470 8864)

" *The beach, the palm trees and people-watching on Ocean Front Walk, plus great shopping and dining, make this one of my favourite haunts.* **"**

Pier pressure Santa Monica's landmark 1909 pier still exudes that old-fashioned amusement-park aura which evokes a fuzzy nostalgia in adults and requests for money from attendant offspring. Along the weathered wooden boardwalk, Pacific Park's (➤ 58) giant Ferris wheel and roller-coaster loom above the restored 1922 carousel operated by Paul Newman in *The Sting*. On the beach below, listen for the 14-foot-high wind harp chairs, part of the Natural Elements Sculpture Park, and rent a bike or in-line skates to swoop along the 22-mile concrete beach path.

Beyond the beach Santa Monica's inland entertainment hub is Third Street Promenade, four pedestrianised blocks of shops, cafés and movie theatres. For a more esoteric experience, check out Main Street (between Hollister and Rose Avenues), with its trendy restaurants and art galleries, and the California Heritage Museum (at Ocean Park), housed in an 1894 residence built for Santa Monica's founder, Senator John Jones (➤ 15).

Venice Beach Where Main crosses Rose Street, Joseph Borofsky's *Ballerina Clown* figure greets visitors to Venice. It is an appropriate icon for this entertaining beach community, a throwback to the psychedelic Sixties combined with the narcissism of Muscle Beach. Ocean Front Walk is where it all hangs out, a non-stop parade of scantily-clad humanity, body-builders, buskers and stalls. A short walk away, the quiet canal-lined residential neighbourhood that gave the area its name can be explored on foot.

THE GETTY CENTER

"One of the most significant cultural events to take place in Los Angeles in 1997 is the opening of the new Getty Center, and I for one will be amongst the first in the queue."

The background Oil billionaire J Paul Getty began collecting in the 1930s, and his particular passion for Greek and Roman antiquities inspired the Roman villa at Malibu (▶ 20), which opened as a museum in 1974. On his death, the J Paul Getty Trust received a billion-dollar endowment and the museum collections boomed, the Trust's massive spending power often causing considerable resentment in the art-buying world. A site was acquired for expansion in the Brentwood Hills, West LA, and plans were drawn up by architect Richard Meier.

Treasure trove While the Getty antiquities remain in Malibu, the rest of the collections are destined for Meier's inside-out museum arranged as a series of pavilions around an outdoor courtyard overlooking the city. The scope and quality of the exhibits is daunting and it is a good idea to concentrate on a couple of areas, such as sculpture or European paintings from the 14th to 19th centuries. There are Old Master drawings; a glittering collection of French decorative arts including clocks, porcelain and silver commissioned for the royal and imperial households; stunning medieval illuminated manuscripts; and photographs by Nadar, Man Ray and Edward Weston. To avoid cultural overload, take a break to explore the gardens and admire the views. Gallery talks are offered daily in the museum, and the Center runs lectures, exhibitions and research projects.

HIGHLIGHTS

- *Entry of the Animals into Noah's Ark*, Breughel the Elder
- *Irises*, van Gogh
- *Ludwig* (illuminated) Manuscripts
- *Portrait of James Christie*, Gainsborough
- *Starry Night*, Munch
- *Still-Life* (wood carving), Parent
- *Venus and Adonis*, Titian
- Photographs by Walker Evans (US, 1903–75)

Top: Coronation of the Virgin, *da Fabriano. Above:* Bacchante, *ter Brugghen*

INFORMATION

- Off map, west
- off I–405/San Diego Freeway
- Restaurant (££) and cafés (£)
- Very good
- Free

ARMAND HAMMER MUSEUM OF ART

HIGHLIGHTS

- Beach at Trouville, Boudin
- Dans l'Omnibus, Vuillard
- Grunwald Center exhibitions
- Hospital at Saint-Rémy, van Gogh
- Mme Hessel at the Seashore, Vuillard
- The Sower, van Gogh
- Street Scene, Bonnard

INFORMATION

- Off map, west
- 10899 Wilshire Boulevard, Westwood
- 310/443 7000
- Tue–Sat 11–7 (Thu 11–9); Sun 11–6. Closed Mon
- Courtyard café (£)
- 20, 21, 22, 320
- Very good
- Inexpensive
- Westwood Village (▶ 18 and 70), UCLA's Franklin D Murphy Sculpture Garden (▶ 59)

Above: Two Actors (Honoré Daumier)
Right: bust of Armand Hammer

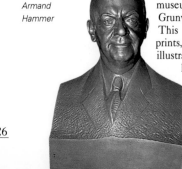

"Roundly criticised for its architecture, the lack of 'importance' of its collections, even for its existence, the Hammer is not a big favourite with the local cultural panjandrums. However, I am rather partial to several small-scale treasures here.**"**

Hammer and tongs Much of the highbrow carping about the Hammer can be traced to sour grapes. The immensely rich and acquisitive Armand Hammer, an oil millionaire many times over, originally promised his art collections to a number of local institutions. When he decided to build his own museum, the news was greeted with dismay.

Minor miracles The modest size of the Hammer is actually a boon after several of the more overwhelming local museums. Its collection largely comprises Impressionist and Post-Impressionist works by such painters as Monet, Pissarro and Mary Cassatt, and complementary works from UCLA's own collections are also shown here.

Changing exhibitions Selections from the 19th-century Daumier and his Contemporaries Collection, featuring paintings, sculpture and lithographs by the leading French satirist of the age, are shown in rotation, and the museum is a showcase for the UCLA Grunwald Center for the Graphic Arts. This collection of more than 35,000 prints, drawings, photographs and book illustrations, containing works by such luminaries as Dürer, Cézanne, Matisse and Jasper Johns, is displayed in frequently changing themed exhibitions. Do check out the museum's visiting exhibitions programme.

BEVERLY HILLS

"Love it or loathe it, I don't believe you can say you have done Los Angeles until you have seen Beverly Hills. The city's most recognisable zip code (90210) receives over 14 million visitors a year, making it the No 1 tourist attraction in Los Angeles."

A star is born In a classic rags-to-riches story, the countrified suburb of Beverly Hills, west of Hollywood, was plucked from obscurity by the movies – Douglas Fairbanks Snr to be exact, who set up home here in 1919.

The Golden Triangle Today, Beverly Hills remains ostentatiously star-studded, a monument to conspicuous consumption. For black-belt window shopping, the 'Golden Triangle', bounded by Crescent Drive, Wilshire and Santa Monica boulevards, is bisected by world-famous Rodeo Drive, a showpiece three-block strip of designer emporia. At the Wilshire Boulevard end, the $200-million 'European-style' Via Rodeo fashion retail complex features real cobblestones, a miniaturised version of Rome's Spanish Steps, and the largest branch of ritzy jewellers Tiffany & Co outside New York City.

Seeing the sights An historical walking tour map of Beverly Hills is available from the Visitors Bureau. The walk takes about an hour and covers such local sights as the imposing City Hall, Beverly Gardens, and the wonderful Gaudí-like O'Neill House, 507 N Rodeo Drive (be sure to nip down the alley to admire the swirling stucco and mosaic inlay of the guest house). If you want to see movie moguls at play, one of the best venues in town is the Polo Lounge at the flamingo pink Beverly Hills Hotel (► 84).

DID YOU KNOW?

- Beverly Hills covers a mere 5.4 square miles
- The average net annual income of Beverly Hills residents is $121,500
- Beverly Hills' 208 licensed beauty, health and hair-styling businesses generate more than $25 million per annum
- The Rodeo Drive boutique featured in Judith Krantz's *Scruples* was based on Fred Hayman, 273 N Rodeo Drive

INFORMATION

Beverly Hills Visitors Bureau
- Off map, west
- 239 S Beverly Drive
- 310/271 8174
- Mon–Fri 8:30–5
- 20, 21, 22, 320

Beverly Hills Trolley Tour
- Rodeo Drive at Dayton Way
- 310/285 2563
- Jul–Sep daily 10:30–5:30, departures every hour on the half hour. Tour duration, 25 minutes
- Inexpensive

- Greystone Park (► 57), Museum of Television and Radio (► 51), Virginia Robinson Gardens (► 57)

5

LA COUNTY MUSEUM OF·ART

HIGHLIGHTS

- Drawings and pastels, Degas
- Edo scrolls and netsuke, Japanese Pavilion
- Moscow Avant-Garde School paintings and drawings (Kandinsky and Rodchenko)
- *Jazz Facsimile*, Matisse
- *La Pipe*, Magritte
- Persian illuminated manuscripts
- *Untitled*, Rothko
- *Waterlilies*, Monet

INFORMATION

- ✚ Off map, west
- ✉ 5905 Wilshire Boulevard, Midtown
- ☎ 213/857 6000
- 🕐 Tue–Thu 10–5; Fri 10–9; Sat–Sun 11–6. Closed Mon, Thanksgiving, Christmas
- 🍴 Plaza Café (£–££)
- 🚌 20, 21, 22, 217, 320
- ♿ Very good
- ✋ Moderate
- ↔ George C Page Museum of La Brea (➤ 50), Farmers' Market (➤ 71), Petersen Automotive Museum (➤ 29)

"*One of the finest, most broad-ranging art museums in the US, LACMA also gets my vote for its alfresco jazz concerts held in the courtyard plaza on Friday evenings and Sunday afternoons.*"

Make a plan The museum complex is spread over five buildings. Its collections are so vast and varied that there is far too much to be seen comfortably in a single visit, so it is advisable to plot a route around personal favourites with the aid of a layout plan (constantly changing) from the information kiosk.

The collections The majority of the permanent collections are housed in the Ahmanson Building. Here, magnificent examples of ancient Asian, Egyptian and pre-Columbian art, medieval and Renaissance paintings, works by 17th-century Dutch landscape specialists and 18th-century French Romantics have been gathered together with a feast of Impressionist, Fauvist, Cubist and Surrealist art. There is a dazzling array of British silver, diverse examples of European and American decorative arts, plus costumes and textiles, jewel-like Persian manuscripts and Ottoman ceramics. The museum boasts world-class collections of 20th-century American and German Expressionist art, and the Bruce Goff Japanese Pavilion is a work of art in itself.

Exhibitions and sculpture gardens In addition to housing selections from the permanent collections, the Anderson and Hammer Buildings offer acres of special exhibition space, and LACMA is a great place to catch top-flight visiting exhibitions. The buildings are flanked by sculpture gardens with works by Rodin, Bourdelle, Calder and Alice Aycock.

Portrait of an Artist (Pool with Two Figures), *David Hockney*

PETERSEN AUTOMOTIVE MUSEUM

❝*What better place to examine the cult of the automobile than Los Angeles, a city entirely shaped by the motor car?*❞

Driving through history The largest museum of its kind in the US, the Petersen explores automotive history and culture from early jalopies through to the sleek dream machines of the Testa Rossa zone. The ground-floor 'Streetscape', a series of dioramas and eye-catching displays designed to illustrate the effects of motoring on people's lives, kicks off with a 1911 American Underslung touring car puffing real steam from its radiator, and continues via a classic Laurel and Hardy scene involving a Ford Model T, to a gleaming 1929 gas station, and a glossy 1930s new car showroom complete with cigar-chomping buyer. L.A. Autotude salutes the automobile as fashion accessory with a selection of bizarre and eccentric cars off the city's streets, and there are tributes to the 1950s and '60s, plus a look at vehicles of the future.

Capital of customising On the second floor, the galleries present a constantly changing feast of automotive excellence: stars' cars in the Hollywood Gallery; LA hot rods from California's capital of customising; and the Otis Chandler Motorcycle Gallery.

Top: diorama of 1911 touring car. Right: car showroom, 1930s

HIGHLIGHTS

- 1957 Ferrari 250 Testa Rossa
- Customised cars from Dean Jeffries and George Barris

INFORMATION

- ✛ Off map, west
- ✉ 6060 Wilshire Boulevard, Midtown
- ☎ 213/930 2277
- 🕐 Tue–Sun 10–6. Closed Mon except holidays
- 🍴 Cafeteria (£)
- 🚌 20, 21, 22, 217, 320
- ♿ Very good
- Moderate
- ↔ George C Page Museum of La Brea (▶ 50), LA County Museum of Art (▶ 28), Farmers' Market (▶ 71)

HOLLYWOOD BOULEVARD

INFORMATION

Visitors Information Center

⊞ El

✉ Janes House, 6541 Hollywood Boulevard, Hollywood

☎ 213/689 8822 (Events Hotline)

🕐 Mon–Sat 9–5. Closed Sun

🚋 1

🎫 Free

↔ Capitol Records Tower (► 54), Hollyhock House (► 34), Hollywood Memorial Park Cemetery (► 52)

Above: Mann's Chinese Theater. Below: the famous hand- and footprints outside it

"Though the stars are long gone, and Hollywood Boulevard's heyday in the 1930s and 1940s is a distant memory, I still get a kick out of inspecting Trigger's hoofprints outside Mann's Chinese Theater."

Facelift After almost 50 years of decay and decline, Tinseltown's most evocative address is in line for a major facelift. One of the first things to be buffed up along the boulevard has been the Hollywood Walk of Fame. Stretching between Gower Street and La Brea Avenue, with an annexe on Vine, almost 2,000 bronze stars set in the sidewalk honour celebrities in film, television, theatre and radio. The select few invited to place their hands, feet, hooves, or (in the case of Betty Grable) legs in the concrete courtyard of Mann's Chinese Theater (►55) include Joan Crawford, James Stewart and Cary Grant. Here, kiosks sell self-guided Hollywood star site maps, but for the best insider guide to Hollywood sleaze, take a Grave Line Tour (►53).

Hollywood history Sid Grauman, who built the Chinese Theater, was also one of the founding partners in the Hollywood Roosevelt Hotel (►53) across the street. A couple of Michelle Pfeiffer's nightclub scenes from *The Fabulous Baker Boys* were filmed here. The celebrity assortment at the Hollywood Wax Museum, 6767 Hollywood Boulevard (until midnight daily), is rather drab. Near by, kids might enjoy the Hollywood Guinness World of Records Museum (►58). There's also the exotic Frederick's of Hollywood Lingerie Museum (►52).

UNIVERSAL STUDIOS

" *The world's biggest and busiest motion picture and television studio–cum–theme park is a great family day out, and I reckon the stunning new Jurassic Park: The Ride adventure may be worth the cost of admission alone.* **"**

Back to the beginning Universal Studios' founder Carl Laemmle moved his movie studio facility to the Hollywood Hills in 1915 and inaugurated Universal Studios tours for a quarter during the silent movie era. The arrival of the talkies put paid to live audiences. In 1964, tram tours began and now circle the huge 415-acre backlot.

Orientation To get the most out of a day at Universal, pick up a copy of the daily schedule listing the various shows and attractions (➤ Highlights) as soon as you arrive. Top of everyone's list is the Backlot Tram Tour which includes close encounters with old banana breath himself in *Kongfrontation*, Jaws snapping his way around Amity Harbor, the ground-trembling *Earthquake: The Big One*, and classic locations from the *Psycho* house to Little Europe. Most of the rides and shows are in the upper level Entertainment Center, which is linked to Studio Center, the business end, by a quarter-mile escalator.

Take a ride Until now, Universal's 1993 *Back to the Future* adventure was the most ambitious ride ever created. Over $100 million later, the Studio's high-tech wizards have surpassed themselves, and *Jurassic Park: The Ride*, a lushly landscaped 6-acre site inhabited by staggeringly realistic dinosaurs, opened in the summer of 1996. Designed with the help of aerospace scientists, these beauties, including the five-storey-high *Ultrasaurus* and sinister, spitting *Dilophosaurus*, can move at speeds of up to 25 feet per second.

HIGHLIGHTS

- *Backdraft*
- *Backlot Tram Tour*
- *Back to the Future – The Ride*
- *Beethoven's Animal Actors Stage*
- *The Flintstones Show*
- *Jurassic Park – The Ride*
- *Star-spotting in the Studio Commissary*
- *WaterWorld – A Live Sea War Spectacular*
- *The Wild, Wild, Wild West Stunt Show*
- *The World of Cinemagic*

INFORMATION

- ✚ Off map, northwest
- ✉ Universal City Drive (off I–101/Hollywood Freeway)
- ☎ 818/622 3801
- 🕐 Daily, summer 8AM–9PM (box office 8–5); winter 9–7 (box office 8–4). Closed Thanksgiving, Christmas
- 🍽 A wide range of dining options and fast food outlets (£–££)
- 🚌 420, 424, 425, 522
- ♿ Good
- 💷 Very expensive (tickets are all-inclusive of rides, shows and attractions); children under 3 free. Moderate parking fees
- ↔ Griffith Park (➤ 32)
- ❓ Regularly scheduled Spanish- and Japanese-language tram tours. French-language tours can be booked ahead

9

GRIFFITH PARK

"There are dozens of good reasons to visit Griffith Park. Amongst my favourites are picnicking in the Ferndell, the Autry Museum (► 33), horse-riding in the hills, and star-gazing of the planetary kind at the Observatory."

A handsome bequest The largest municipal park in the US, Griffith Park lies in the foothills of the Santa Monica Mountains. The original 3,015-acre site was given to the city in 1896 by Col Griffith Jenkins Griffith, who also left a trust with sufficient funds to build the amphitheatre-style Greek Theatre, a favourite outdoor concert venue, and the landmark Griffith Observatory overlooking the city. The copper-domed observatory houses an astronomy museum. There are daily planetarium and laserium shows, plus free admission to inspect the heavens through a giant Zeiss telescope on clear evenings.

Around the park The huge park offers a tremendous variety of scenery. You can walk the cool, leafy Ferndell trail or reach the rugged high chaparral by a network of walking trails and bridle paths (maps from the Ranger Station). In the southeast corner of the park, there are miniature train rides and children's pony rides near the Los Feliz exit. The antique merry-go-round, near the Ranger Station, is another hot favourite with small children, and there are picnic areas, 28 tennis courts and four golf courses (► 83) with plenty of convenient parking. The Los Angeles Zoo offers 77 landscaped acres of animal enclosures and shows. Near by, the Los Angeles Equestrian Center rents out American quarter horses. The central Ranger Station can also supply a list of stables in the park area, including Sunset Ranch (☎ 213/464 9612), which offers escorted moonlit night rides.

AUTRY MUSEUM OF WESTERN HERITAGE

"This spirited and entertaining celebration of all things Western appeals to young and old alike – and it's hard to walk away without secretly coveting a Stetson, or at least a bandanna from the museum store."

The singing cowboy Housed in a California Mission-style complex, the museum is named for Gene Autry, the singing cowboy of Hollywood Western fame. The Autry Foundation was a prime mover in the establishment of the museum, which tells the story of the West through its magnificent collections of artefacts – over 40,000 individual pieces.

Winning the West The museum's seven galleries provide a riveting insight into American Western history and heritage beginning with the Spanish age of discovery. The wagon-train era exhibit is enlivened by extracts from pioneer diaries, while real gold nuggets add a frisson of authenticity to tales of the California Gold Rush, and the Spirit of the Community gallery explores European, Mexican and Chinese migration in the Old West. Meet the gunslingers – and the guns they slung – plus the Spanish *vaqueros* who were herding cattle on horseback for 300 years before the emergence of Mexican *charros*, the cowboys of popular imagery. Children get to dress up in boots and spurs for a romp around the Children's Discovery Gallery, and then move on to the Spirit of Imagination Gallery for an intelligent look at Western culture as portrayed on screen.

HIGHLIGHTS

- Colt Firearms Collection
- Early art from the West
- Frederick Remington's bronze statues
- Indian beadwork and folk crafts
- Listening to the pioneer diaries
- Trails West environmental display
- Western film and television memorabilia

INFORMATION

- ✚ Off map, northwest
- ✉ 4700 Western Heritage Way, Griffith Park (junction of I–5/Golden State Freeway and 134/Ventura Freeway)
- ☎ 213/667 2000
- ◷ Tue–Sun 10–5. Closed Mon, Thanksgiving, Christmas
- 🍴 Golden Spur Café (£–££)
- 🚌 96
- ♿ Excellent
- 💷 Moderate
- ↔ Griffith Park (➤ 32), Universal Studios (➤ 31)
- ❓ Frequent special exhibitions

33

HOLLYHOCK HOUSE

DID YOU KNOW?

- Built for: Aline Barnsdall (1882–1946)
- Designed by: Frank Lloyd Wright (1867–1959)
- Assisted by: Rudolph Schindler (1887–1953)
- Construction: 1919–21
- Chief building materials: pre-cast concrete, oak, glass
- Donated to the city: 1927

INFORMATION

- ✚ H2
- ✉ Barnsdall Park, 4800 Hollywood Boulevard, Hollywood
- ☎ 213/662 7272
- 🕐 Tue–Sat, tours at noon, 1, 2, 3. Closed Mon
- 🚌 1
- ♿ None
- 💵 Inexpensive

The Hollyhock's interior

" Set on a small, green mound in the Hollywood flatlands, Frank Lloyd Wright's Hollyhock House is not only one of LA's most prestigious architectural treasures, it is a great place for a picnic, with sweeping views across the city. "

Olive Hill Oil heiress Aline Barnsdall originally commissioned Wright to design a full-scale theatrical community on Olive Hill, but financial and artistic differences brought the project to an end with only three buildings completed.

'Organic' design Hollyhock House crowns the crest of the hill, and is named for Barnsdall's favourite flower which appears in abstract form in the dramatic Mayan-style geometric reliefs and pinnacles which adorn the squat concrete building. Part-temple, part-California Bungalow, Wright's 'organic' design deliberately connects each significant interior space with its neighbour and with a related exterior space so clear progressive sight lines are established, and a sense of light and air predominates. The spatial complexity of the interior, with its raised and lowered floor and ceiling levels, is contrasted with a relaxing autumnal colour scheme and the simplicity of the materials – cement and wood. The wonderful roofscape was also designed as an integral extension of the living space.

Design dictator Though often absent, Wright employed several cunning devices to ensure his vision was adhered to. Canted walls prevented pictures being hung in the bedrooms, and extra wide baseboards also meant no furniture could be placed against the walls. However, the young overseeing architect, Rudolph Schindler (▶ 56), managed to slip in a few of his own ideas, including the wonderful locks on the front door.

NATURAL HISTORY MUSEUM

"This is one of the most enjoyable natural history museums I have ever visited, and there is far more to be seen here than the usual array of stuffed birds, beasts and prehistoric relatives."

The broad picture The museum's home is a handsome Spanish Renaissance Revival affair on the north side of Exposition Park. Its collections cover an enormous amount of ground and in addition to the natural history exhibits there are superb Mesoamerican artefacts including gold jewellery and pottery from the Maya, Inca and Aztec cultures; an excellent Native American Indian section with a re-created pueblo, intricate Plains Indian beadwork and Navajo textiles; and California and American history galleries.

Natural wonders Much to the delight of *Jurassic Park* fans, the County Museum is BIG on fossils and dinosaurs. This is the place to ogle a *Sauropod*, a pin-headed 72-foot-long giant and one of the largest dinosaurs ever discovered. It probably weighed around 30–40 tons, dwarfing *Tyrannosaurus rex* (a mere 50 feet long and 6–7 tons). *Carnotaurus*, the meat-eating monster first discovered in Patagonia in 1984, also puts in an appearance, as does the rhino-like *Brontops*, or 'Thunderbeast'. There is a glittering Hall of Gems and Minerals to admire; and the giant dioramas of African and North American mammals are terrific. Do not miss the brilliant Discovery Center. Children will love the imaginative touchy-feely games and toys, fossil rubbings and other hands-on diversions. On the mezzanine level, the Insect Zoo offers a suitably creepy-crawly collection of slumbering scorpions, huge hissing cockroaches from Madagascar, pink-toed tarantulas and nauseating assassin bugs.

DID YOU KNOW?

- The total weight of a swarm of African locusts: 300 million pounds (1,500 tons)
- The Jurassic fish with teeth longer than a great white shark: *Xiphactonus audax*
- The world's deepest natural diver: Emperor penguin (840 feet)
- World's fastest diver: peregrine falcon (180mph)
- The famous US prison named for a bird: Alcatraz (Spanish for pelican)
- The two biggest bird stars of jungle movie soundtracks: the Australian kookaburra and Indian blue peafowl

INFORMATION

- J11
- 900 Exposition Boulevard
- 213/744 DINO (3466)
- Museum Tue–Sun 10–5; Discovery Center Tue–Fri 10–3, Sat–Sun 10–4. Closed Mon (except for museum on national holidays), Thanksgiving, Christmas, New Year's Day
- Cafeteria (£)
- 40, 42, 81; DASH C/Expo Park
- Very good
- Moderate

13

WELLS FARGO HISTORY MUSEUM

DID YOU KNOW?

- Average speed of a Concord Stagecoach: 5mph
- Number of horses: 6 (changed every 12 miles)
- Duration of journey from Omaha to Sacramento: 15 days
- Cost: $300
- Baggage limit: 25lb per person
- Pony Express: operational April 1860 to October 1861
- Original route (duration): St Joseph, Mo, to Sacramento, CA (1,966 miles in 10–12 days)
- Total mail carried: 35,000 letters

INFORMATION

- ✚ M7
- ✉ 333 S Grand Avenue
- ☎ 213/253 7166
- 🕐 Mon–Fri 9–5. Closed Sat–Sun
- 🚌 DASH B
- ♿ Good
- 🎟 Free
- ↔ Biltmore Hotel (➤ 56), California Plaza (➤ 54), Los Angeles Central Library (➤ 56), Museum of Contemporary Art (➤ 37), Grand Central Market (➤ 38)

"An Old West legend right up there with the Colt Six-Shooter, Wyatt Earp and 'Buffalo Bill' Cody, Wells Fargo celebrates the company's rip-roaring early history with tales of the Forty-Niners, the Pony Express and Concord Stagecoaches."

Expanding west By 1852, when Henry Wells and William G Fargo set up their Western banking and express service in San Francisco, the California Gold Rush was in full swing. The new venture swiftly established a reputation for buying, selling and transporting gold and valuables. In the early 1860s, Wells, Fargo & Co took over the western leg of the famed Pony Express. They operated a stagecoach service from the 1860s, and were among the first to take to the rails when the transcontinental railroad was completed in 1869.

'Cradle on Wheels' Pride of place in the museum goes to an original Concord Stagecoach, named for its birthplace in Concord, Mass. Though Mark Twain romantically described it as a 'cradle on wheels', the reality of a stagecoach journey was far from relaxing. Up to 18 passengers, including the driver and guard, could be squeezed into the nine-seat leather upholstered interior and on to the open-air upper deck. Stops were infrequent, the food barely edible, and aside from the constant jolting, dust and discomfort, perils of the road included highwaymen and frequent accidents. Among the numerous artefacts on display, there is no missing the plum-sized gold nugget found in California's Feather River, near Challenge, in 1975. This 26.4oz lucky find was worth around $15,000. Another eye-catcher is a 7,500lb, 19th-century safe handpainted with pastoral scenes and flowers which were supposed to allay customers' concerns.

MUSEUM OF CONTEMPORARY ART

❝One museum with two addresses a mile apart, MOCA's growing catalogue of post-1940 artworks is now one of the most important contemporary art collections in the US.❞

Downtown All blonde wood and vast white spaces, MOCA's Downtown galleries, designed by Japanese architect Arata Isozaki, present frequently changing exhibitions including works from the permanent collection. The busy calendar also introduces visiting exhibits and newly commissioned projects and works by established and emerging artists.

Across town While Isozaki's museum was under construction, MOCA transformed a spacious warehouse building in Little Tokyo into gallery space, now known as the Geffen Contemporary at MOCA. The vast industrial space with its ramps and girders is ideal for big installation pieces as well as smaller works which occupy a maze of galleries overlooked from a mezzanine level. In an interesting display designed to provide a loose comparative time-frame for contemporary art, a series of four 'context rooms' note major historical, political and artistic developments since the 1940s in chronological order.

HIGHLIGHTS

Works by:
- De Kooning
- Giacometti
- Mondrian
- Pollock
- Oldenburg

INFORMATION

MOCA
- ✚ M7
- ✉ 250 S Grand Avenue
- ☎ 213/626 6222
- 🕐 Tue–Sun 11–5 (Thu until 8). Closed Mon, Thanksgiving, Christmas, New Year's Day
- 🍴 Patinette at MOCA (£–££)
- 🚌 DASH B
- ♿ Good
- 🎟 Moderate (includes both buildings); free on Thu after 5
- ↔ Biltmore Hotel (➤ 56), California Plaza (➤ 54), Los Angeles Central Library (➤ 56), Wells Fargo History Museum (➤ 36)
- ❓ Regularly scheduled art talks programme, free with museum admission (information, ☎ 213/621 1757)

Geffen Contemporary
- ✚ N7
- ✉ 152 N Central Avenue
- 🚌 DASH A
- ↔ Japanese-American National Museum (➤ 50), Little Tokyo (➤ 40)

Unusual exhibit outside the MOCA

15

GRAND CENTRAL MARKET

"For a self-confessed market lover, Downtown's colourful produce market is a real find. As well as providing a feast for the eyes, it is also a great place to grab picnic makings or stop for a snack."

Downtown's historic larder LA's largest and oldest food market first opened its doors in 1917, and the hanger-like building, with entrances on both Broadway and Hill Street, has been feeding the Downtown district ever since. In those days, Broadway was LA's poshest thoroughfare, while today it is the heart of LA's crowded Hispanic shopping district, which steps up several gears from busy to seething on Saturdays when the noise and the bustle in the market is unbelievable.

Capsicums and cacti Coming from the street into the market and its maze of closely packed stalls is like entering a foodie version of Aladdin's Cave. There is sawdust on the floor, the chop-chop of butcher's knives thud away on a dozen counters, and you are met by a vision of glossy piles of massed capsicums, avocados and big beefy tomatoes, stooks of celery, colour-coded potatoes, huge bunches of bananas, pyramids of oranges, lemons, limes and apples. Among the less familiar offerings are prickly pears and cactus leaves, dozens of different types of fresh and dried chillies available in varying degrees of ferocity, and the Mexican butchers display bits of beasts one would rather not even think about (vegetarians avoid this area). There are more than 50 stalls in all including fish merchants and bakers, confectioners, delicatessens selling cheese and cold meats, spice merchants, dried fruit and nut sellers, and the Chinese herbal medicine man. Take-away food stalls do a roaring trade in Mexican specialities, and there are snack stops with tables and chairs near the Hill Street exit.

BRADBURY BUILDING

"Just across the street from the hubbub of Grand Central Market, the Bradbury is a hidden treasure. Not only is it an architectural gem, quite literally one-of-a-kind, but its bizarre history is intriguing."

A millionaire's monument In 1892, elderly mining millionaire Lewis Bradbury invited an obscure architect's draftsman, 32-year-old George Wyman, to submit designs for a building to act as a monument to his achievements. Wyman initially refused, but one evening as he sat at a ouija-board with his wife, they received a message from his dead brother, which read 'Take the Bradbury building. It will make you famous.' Spurred on by this occult communication, and inspired by Edward Bellamy's 1887 science fiction novel *Looking Backward*, which actually looked forward to life in a Utopian society in the year 2000, Wyman created a dazzling futuristic building which would cost Bradbury more than three times the initial estimates but rank among the marvels of the age.

From fiction to fact The Bradbury's Italianate façade is attractive but unexceptional. However, once through the door and into the soaring, light-filled atrium the vista is amazing. Light pours down through the narrow well, drawing the eye immediately upward and dramatising the sensation of height. Against a backdrop of golden-yellow tiles, pink glazed brick and polished wood, intricate, black wrought-iron railings edge the balconies and flights of marble steps climb five storeys to the roof. Though Wyman took a correspondence course in architecture after he completed the Bradbury, he never designed another significant building. Unfortunately Lewis Bradbury died just before his monument was opened in 1893.

DID YOU KNOW?

- Cost: $500,000
- Marble: Belgian
- Railings: French (displayed at the 1893 Chicago World Fair)
- Tiles: Mexican
- Wood: oak
- Uses: commercial offices and film shoots (notably *Bladerunner*, starring Harrison Ford)

INFORMATION

- ✚ M7
- ✉ 304 S Broadway (access to the hallway only)
- ☎ 213/626 1893
- 🕐 Mon–Sat 9–5. Closed Sun
- Ⓜ Civic Center
- 🚌 DASH D
- ♿ None
- 🎫 Free
- ↔ Biltmore Hotel (➤ 56), California Plaza (➤ 54), Grand Central Market (➤ 38), Museum of Contemporary Art (➤ 37), Wells Fargo History Museum (➤ 36)

LITTLE TOKYO

> *"The hub of LA's 200,000-strong Japanese-American community, Little Tokyo is pleasantly low-key and walkable. There are surprise outposts of Japanese landscaping tucked into the concrete jungle, and plenty of craft shops to nose around."*

Historical footnotes Bounded by First and Third, Los Angeles and San Pedro streets, this area was first settled at the tail end of the 19th century, and several historic buildings remain on First Street, which leads down to the Japanese-American National Museum (► 50).

Sushi **and** *shiatsu* Amongst the neat green pom-poms of pollarded trees and bright blue tile roofs, Japanese Village Plaza's 40 restaurants and small shops, exotic supermarkets, *sushi* bars and *shiatsu* massage parlours make for interesting browsing. Across Second Street the Japanese-American Cultural and Community Center houses the Doizaki Gallery's exhibits of Japanese artworks; the adjacent theatre is used for contemporary and traditional Japanese performances such as Noh plays and Kabuki theatre productions. On the plaza, a huge stone memorial commemorates the *Issei* (first generation Japanese-Americans).

Garden oasis In the far corner, search out the delightful little James Irvine Garden. This Japanese-style oasis is encircled by a burbling stream, and there are paths and bridges, stepping stones, trees and flowering shrubs such as azaleas. There is more elegant Japanese landscaping near by, outside the Higashi Hongwanji Buddhist Temple, 505 E Third Street, where dwarf pines, grassy tuffets and rock arrangements front the graceful neo-traditional façade.

EL PUEBLO DE LOS ANGELES

"Though this historic city park is a favourite tourist destination, Angelenos tend to be a bit snooty about its rampant commercialism. However, I for one enjoy sampling such local diversions as Sunday's mariachi masses in the Old Plaza Church."

LA's historic heart Wedged between Chinatown and Downtown, the site of the original 1781 pueblo settlement covers just a handful of city blocks. Within its confines are 27 historic buildings, including two museums, restaurants, shops and a Mexican street market. The main thoroughfare is pedestrianised Olvera Street, leading off La Placita, the former town plaza shaded by Moreton Bay fig trees. On the south side of the plaza, free guided walking tours (🕐 Tue–Sat 10, 11, noon, 1) leave from a low brick building alongside the original 1884 Firehouse No 1, which displays antique fire-fighting equipment. The Old Plaza Church, on the west side, is the city's oldest Catholic church, dedicated in 1822.

Sterling support One of the oldest streets in the city, Olvera Street fell into disrepair around the turn of the century when the Downtown area moved south. By 1926, it was a grimy, mud-filled alley until Christine Sterling stepped in. The story of Sterling's campaign to rescue the historic buildings and inaugurate the market is told in a display at the restored Avila Adobe.

Mexican marketplace Across the street, the Visitors Center in the 1887 Sepulveda House distributes walking tour maps, and shows a short video history of the city. The market founded in the 1930s is still going strong, and the crowded thoroughfare is bursting with dozens of market stalls selling everything from Mexican pottery to souvenir sombreros.

DID YOU KNOW?

- Original settlement: Pueblo de Nuestra Señora la Reina de los Angeles (Our Lady Queen of the Angels)
- Oldest existing building: Avila Adobe (1818)
- The adobe (mud) walls of the Avila House are 3 feet thick
- The Avila House served as headquarters for Commodore Robert Stockton of the US Army during the Mexican-American War
- The Moreton Bay fig trees on the plaza were planted in the 1870s

INFORMATION

Visitors Center

- ✚ N6
- ✉ W-12 Olvera Street
- ☎ 213/628 1274
- 🕐 Mon–Sat 9–5. Closed Sun
- 🚌 DASH B, D
- ♿ Few
- 💲 Free
- ↔ Chinatown (▶ 17), Union Station (▶ 56)
- ❓ Cinco de Mayo (5 May) and Dia de los Muertos (2 Nov) festivals (▶ 22)

Plaza Firehouse and Avila Adobe Museums

- 🕐 Tue–Sat 10–3. Closed Sun–Mon
- 💲 Free

19

LONG BEACH AND THE *QUEEN MARY*

" *An easy day trip south from central Los Angeles, Long Beach offers a clutch of diverse sights, good shopping and dining.* **"**

Downtown to Venice Island Starting from Downtown's Pine Avenue, a popular retail and restaurant quarter, E Ocean Boulevard runs along San Pedro Bay. Here the attractive Long Beach Museum of Art, 2300 E Ocean Boulevard (☎ 310/439 2119), is housed in a 1912 Craftsman-style residence with a sculpture garden overlooking the water. The four-mile-long golden sand beach at Belmont Shores is well-supplied with concessionaires renting out boogie boards, kayaks and sailboats, as well as bikes and skates for riding the beach path. Behind the beach, Second Street is home to a mixed bag of shops and restaurants, and crosses on to Naples Island. This affluent residential neighbourhood criss-crossed with canals was developed in the 1920s. It can be explored on foot, or take a ride with Gondola Getaway (▶ 19).

On the water South of Downtown, Shoreline Village is a popular shopping and dining spot with boat trips (▶ 19) and fine views of the *Queen Mary* across the harbour. Inland from the Village, look out for Long Beach Arena encircled by the world's biggest mural, *Planet Ocean*, by marine artist Wyland. The *Queen Mary* finally came to rest in Long Beach in 1967. This grand old lady remains the largest liner afloat, and although she has been converted into a hotel, there are self-guided and regular guided tours. The latter are recommended for access to cabin suites, gorgeous art deco salons and other off-limits treats.

RANCHO LOS ALAMITOS

"Often overlooked by visitors to Long Beach, to my mind this historic California ranch house has something for just about everyone. There are delightful gardens, family rooms to inspect, farmyard animals and entertaining special programmes on selected weekends."

Spanish land grant Tucked away behind the gates of an exclusive residential development (not far from Long Beach), the ranch house was once master of all it surveyed. The original 28,500-acre rancho was part of an enormous land allocated to a Spanish soldier, Manuel Nieto, in 1790. The Bixby family took possession of the property in 1881, and the house remained in the family for almost a century until it was donated to the City of Long Beach in 1968.

A family home The Bixbys were one of Southern California's most prominent pioneer ranching families, and Los Alamitos was Fred Bixby's family home. From humble beginnings as a remote adobe shelter, the comfortable ranch house spread out on its hilltop site, and the views stretched across wheatfields to the ocean. During the 1920s–30s, Florence, Fred's wife, set about developing the gardens, which are one of the highlights of the property today. There is a distinctly Mexican-Mediterranean feel to the low white-washed walls and shaded walkways. Look for the lovely rose garden, an impressively spiky cacti collection and a native Californian area. Tours of the house reveal that the original furnishings and family portraits are still in place. Five turn-of-the-century barns house a black-smith's shop, tackroom and stables with Shire draft horses. Children will enjoy inspecting the sheep and goats, ducks, chickens, rabbits and doves.

DID YOU KNOW?

- Original adobe structure: c 1800
- Original Spanish land grant: 300,000 acres
- Present size: 7.5 acres
- Elevation: 40 feet above sea level
- Fred Bixby (1875–1952)
- Florence Green Bixby (1875–1961)
- Biggest tree: Moreton Bay fig planted 1881

INFORMATION

- ✚ Off map, southeast
- ✉ 6400 Bixby Hill Road (7th Street East; left on Studebaker Road; left on Anaheim)
- ☎ 310/431 3541
- 🕐 Wed–Sun 1–5 (last tour at 4)
- 🚌 LBT 42
- ♿ Few
- 💲 Free
- ↔ Long Beach and the *Queen Mary* (➤ 42)
- ❓ Call for information about events and monthly Sunday afternoon education programmes (mostly free)

GAMBLE HOUSE

HIGHLIGHTS

- Front entrance, leaded glass by Emil Lange
- Main staircase
- Sitting room, carved reliefs of birds and plants
- Rugs from Greene and Greene designs
- Dining room furniture
- Tricks of the butler's pantry
- Guest bedroom, maple furnishings inlaid with silver
- Did you know: the word bungalow is derived from the Hindi word 'bangla', a single-storey house with thatched roof covering the surrounding veranda?

INFORMATION

"The Gamble House takes the utilitarian California Bungalow and turns it into an art form. To my mind, every impeccably handcrafted inch of this superb American Arts and Craft Movement house is a masterpiece."

The California Bungalow The Gamble House was built for David and Mary Gamble (of Procter and Gamble fame) by the architectural firm of Greene and Greene in 1908. Brothers Charles and Henry Greene produced a handful of luxurious wooden 'bungalows' in the first decade of the century of which this is the most complete and well preserved. The informal bungalow-style residence represented an appealing escape from Victorian stuffiness, and it was swiftly translated into Southern California's architectural vernacular.

A symphony in wood The Gamble House is, however, far from being a traditional bungalow. Greene and Greene's spreading two-storey design, with its Japanese-influenced lines, was planned in meticulous detail. The site was chosen to catch cool breezes from the Arroyo, and the arrangement of spacious verandas shaded by second-storey sleeping porches and overhanging eaves keeps the house comfortably ventilated through the summer. Working largely in wood, the Greenes cloaked the exterior with shingles and created a rich, golden timbered interior using Burmese teak, oak, maple, redwood and cedar hand-buffed to a satin-smooth finish. Every fixture and fitting, from the dining room furniture to the andirons in the fireplace, was custom-built, and many of the schemes were designed to complement Mary Gamble's favourite possessions such as Tiffany table lamps and opalescent Rockwood pottery. After your tour have a browse in the museum bookshop.

NORTON SIMON MUSEUM OF ART

"If you have time to visit only one art museum in Los Angeles, I would nominate the Norton Simon. Though less well known than the Getty Center (▶ 25), or LACMA (▶ 28), the range and quality of the collections gathered here are in many ways superior to both."

Industrialist and collector The collections were originally founded as the Pasadena Art Institute in 1924. From the 1960s, under the direction of wealthy industrialist and collector Norton Simon (1907–93), the museum has grown into a world-class collection of European Old Master, Impressionist and Post-Impressionist works and sculpture.

The collections The collections begin with jewel-like 14th-century Italian religious paintings and Renaissance art. The ravishing *Branchini Madonna* is just one of the highlights; the collection includes works by Filippino Lippi, Botticelli, Bellini and Cranach. From the 17th and 18th centuries there are Rembrandt portraits, Canaletto's minutely detailed Venetian scenes drawn with a master draftsman's skill, soft, plump Tiepolo figures and Rubens' oils on an heroic scale. The superb 19th- to 20th-century galleries boast major works by Monet, Renoir, Cézanne and van Gogh, and a fistful of colour from Matisse, Kandinsky, Braque and Klee. The exceptional Degas Collection numbers more than 100 pieces including rare landscapes, enigmatic monotypes and an exceptional series of bronze dancers posthumously cast from wax models found in the artist's studio after his death. If this were not enough, the museum also possesses a rich collection of Hindu and Buddhist sculpture from Nepal, India, Thailand and Cambodia.

HIGHLIGHTS

- *Branchini Madonna,* Giovanni di Paolo
- *Presumed Portrait of the Artist's Son, Titus,* Rembrandt
- *Self-Portrait,* de la Tour
- *The Stonebreakers,* Seurat
- *Exotic Landscape,* Rousseau
- *Flower Vendor,* Rivera
- *Odalisque with Tambourine,* Matisse
- *The Mulberry Tree,* van Gogh (below)
- *Woman with Book,* Picasso
- Degas Collection

INFORMATION

- ✚ Off map, northeast
- ✉ 411 W Colorado Boulevard, Pasadena
- ☎ 818/449 6840
- ◔ Thu–Sun noon–6. Closed Mon–Wed
- ▤ 180, 181, 402
- ♿ Good
- 🎟 Inexpensive
- ↔ Descanso Gardens (▶ 57)

45

23

THE HUNTINGTON

Above: Sarah Siddons as the Tragic Muse (*Sir Joshua Reynolds*)

❝Three separate elements – manuscripts, paintings and the gardens – contribute to the famously rich and varied Huntington experience, and I find there hardly seems enough time to do each of them justice.❞

A specialist collector Railroad tycoon Henry E Huntington (1850–1927) moved to Los Angeles in 1902, and made a second fortune organising the city's inter-urban rail system. When he retired to devote himself to his library, he married his uncle's widow, Arabella Huntington, who encouraged his interest in art. Together they amassed the core collections of 18th-century British portraits and French furnishings and decorative arts.

Manuscripts and portraits The Library's extraordinary treasury of rare and precious manuscripts and books spans 800 years, from the famous 13th-century Ellesmere Chaucer to handwritten drafts of novels and poems by William Blake, Walt Whitman and Jack London amongst others. The 1910 Beaux-Arts mansion, by Myron Hunt and Elmer Grey, displays the famous portrait collection including Gainsborough's *Blue Boy*. Ornate French furnishings and porcelain can also be admired here, and European paintings added to the collection since Huntington's day. The Virginia Steele Scott Gallery houses recent acquisitions of American art from the 18th to early 20th centuries, and furnishings from the Arts and Crafts Movement team of Greene and Greene (➤ 44).

Glorious gardens Huntington began work on the spectacular 130-acre gardens in collaboration with William Hertrich in 1904. Today, there are 15 separate garden areas harbouring around 14,000 different types of plants and trees. The camellia woods are at the height of their beauty in spring, the rose garden in summer.

LA STATE & COUNTY ARBORETUM

❝*Set against the backdrop of the San Gabriel Mountains, these lovely gardens in a corner of the old Rancho Santa Anita offer year-round colour and interest. I find them a great place to unwind.*❞

Mexican rancho Rancho Santa Anita, dating from the 1840s, was one of several ranches in the valley when Hugo Reid built his adobe house here. Silver mining millionaire E J 'Lucky' Baldwin purchased the property in 1875, and constructed a fairy-tale Queen Anne guest house. It is a favourite film location and the gardens have featured in numerous films and TV series requiring exotic locations.

From *Acacia to Ziziphus* The lush profusion of trees and plants includes exuberant jungle areas, towering palms, splashing waterfalls and quiet corners to enjoy the peace – as long as the raucous peacocks are silent. Seek out the aquatic garden, the tropical greenhouse, the demonstration gardens and the California landscape area which shows the valley's natural state. There is so much to see, consider taking a tram tour to the further reaches of the grounds.

DID YOU KNOW?

- Size: 127 acres
- Number of plants: 36,000
- Number of species: 5,000
- Resources: herbarium, library, plant information service
- California Historic Landmark: 1839 Hugo Reid Adobe (15,000-plus hand-made adobe bricks)
- Other historic buildings: 1881 Queen Anne Cottage, 1890 Santa Anita Railroad Depot

INFORMATION

- ✛ Off map, northeast
- ✉ 301 N Baldwin Road, Arcadia (off I–210/Foothill Freeway)
- ☎ 818/821 3222
- ⏱ Daily 9–5 (last ticket sales 4:30). Closed Christmas
- 🍴 Coffee shop selling light refreshments (£)
- 🚌 78, 79, 268
- ♿ Few
- 👁 Moderate
- ↔ Gamble House (➤ 44), Huntington Library, Art Collections and Botanical Gardens (➤ 46), Norton Simon Museum of Art (➤ 45), Old Pasadena (➤ 18)
- ❓ Tram tours (regular departures) visit the extensive grounds

The delightful Queen Anne guest house

25

DISNEYLAND

HIGHLIGHTS

- Adventureland Jungle Cruise
- Big Thunder Mountain Railroad
- Fantasmic! Night-time Spectacular
- Haunted Mansion
- Indiana Jones Adventure
- Matterhorn Bobsleds
- Pirates of the Caribbean
- Roger Rabbit's Car Toon Spin
- Splash Mountain
- Star Tours

INFORMATION

- ✚ Off map, southeast
- ✉ 1313 Harbor Boulevard (off I–5/Santa Ana Freeway), Anaheim
- ☎ 714/999 4565
- ◷ Daily. Call for schedules; approximate hours peak season, 9am–midnight or 1am; low season, Mon–Fri 10–6; Sat–Sun 9–midnight
- 🍴 Snack bars, cafés and restaurants (£–£££)
- 🚌 460
- ♿ Excellent
- 💷 Very expensive (all rides and shows inclusive)
- ❓ Call ahead for details of night-time shows and special holiday events

Top: Sleeping Beauty's Castle

❝ *The uninviting urban sprawl surrounding Disneyland prompted Walt to buy up a chunk of Florida the size of Manhattan to house Walt Disney World. However, once through the gates of this mother and father of all theme parks, the Disney dream remains intact and enduringly popular.* **❞**

Magic Kingdom Since it first opened its doors in 1955, Disneyland has become a worldwide phenomenon. Brilliantly conceived and operated like Swiss clockwork, Disney's particular brand of fantasy combined with good clean fun appeals across almost all age and cultural barriers to the child in (just about) everyone. The 85-acre Magic Kingdom park is divided into eight individually themed 'lands'. The gates open on to Main Street USA, a pastiche Victorian street lined with stores, which leads to the hub of the park at Sleeping Beauty's Castle. From here you can explore the tropically inspired Adventureland, with several of the best rides, take a turn around Wild West-style Frontierland, or visit animal-folksy Critter Country. Small children tend to favour the scaled-down rides in Fantasyland and Mickey's Toontown, while the 'white-knuckle' brigade can get to grips with the $50-million Indiana Jones Adventure.

Think ahead Getting the best out of a trip to Disneyland calls for a little advance planning. During the peak summer season (July to early September) and holiday periods, the park is very crowded and queues for the rides can be an hour long. Weekends are especially busy, though Sundays tend to be better than Saturdays. Veterans arrive early (the ticket office opens 30 minutes before the park) and make a dash for their favourite rides (▶Highlights).

LOS ANGELES'
best

Museums

La Brea tar pits

Oozing from a fissure in the earth's crust, these gooey black tar pits are one of the world's most famous fossil sites. For thousands of years plants, birds and animals have been trapped and entombed here turning the asphalt into a palaeontological soup from which scientists have recovered millions of fossilised remnants from some 420 species of animal and 140 types of plant. Most of the fossils date from 10,000–40,000 years ago.

The splendid glass dome of the Natural History Museum of Los Angeles County

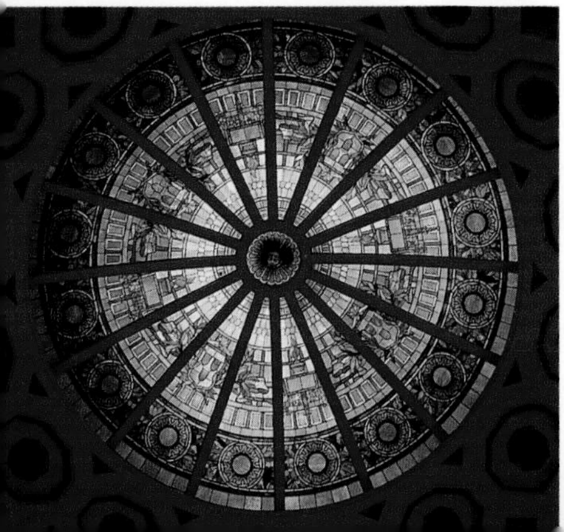

See Top 25 Sights for
AUTRY MUSEUM OF WESTERN HERITAGE (➤ 33)
THE GETTY CENTER (➤ 25)
LOS ANGELES COUNTY MUSEUM OF ART (➤ 28)
MUSEUM OF CONTEMPORARY ART (➤ 37)
NATURAL HISTORY MUSEUM OF LOS ANGELES COUNTY (➤ 35)
NORTON SIMON MUSEUM OF ART (➤ 45)
PETERSEN AUTOMOTIVE MUSEUM (➤ 29)
ARMAND HAMMER MUSEUM OF ART (➤ 26)
WELLS FARGO HISTORY MUSEUM (➤ 36)

BANNING RESIDENCE MUSEUM
Entrepreneur and 'father of Los Angeles transportation', Phineas Banning (1830–85) built this grand Greek Revival mansion in 1864. Splendid Colonial furnishings, a 19th-century carriage barn and park for picnicking.
Off map, south 401 East M Street, Wilmington (off I–110/Harbor Freeway) 310/548 7777 Tue–Thu 12:30–2:30; Sat–Sun 12:30–3:30; closed Mon, Fri; tours on the hour 232 None Inexpensive

GEORGE C PAGE MUSEUM OF LA BREA DISCOVERIES
Built with children in mind, this fascinating museum displays fossilised finds from the La Brea tar pits including a 12-foot-tall Imperial Mammoth skeleton (➤ panel for details).
Off map, west 5801 Wilshire Boulevard, Midtown 213/936 2230 Tue–Sun 10–5 20, 21, 22, 217, 320 Good Moderate

JAPANESE-AMERICAN NATIONAL MUSEUM
The story of Japanese migration to the US, and the Japanese-Americans' struggle for acceptance in their adopted home. Particularly moving exhibits deal with the World War II isolation camps.
N7 369 E First Street 213/625 0414 Tue–Sun 10–5; Thu until 8 DASH A Good Inexpensive

LOS ANGELES MARITIME MUSEUM
The largest maritime museum on the Pacific coast overlooks the busy

Port of Los Angeles. In addition to dozens of beautifully crafted model ships, art and seafaring artefacts, there are real ships to visit.

➕ Off map, south ✉ Berth 84 (end of 6th Street), San Pedro ☎ 310/548 7618 🕐 Tue–Sun 10–5 🚌 447 ♿ Good 💰 Inexpensive

MUSEUM OF NEON ART

This one-of-a-kind museum displays vintage and contemporary neon signs and sculptures, and offers monthly night-time tours of LA's finest neon.

➕ L8 ✉ 501 W Olympic Boulevard ☎ 213/489 9918 🕐 Tue–Sat 11–6; Sun noon–5; Thu until 8 🚌 DASH C, E ♿ Few 💰 Inexpensive

MUSEUM OF SCIENCE AND INDUSTRY

Dozens of child-friendly hands-on displays in the new ScienCenter and Aerospace Hall, plus an IMAX movie theatre.

➕ J11 ✉ Exposition Boulevard at Figueroa ☎ 213/744 7400 🕐 Daily 10–5 🚌 DASH C/Expo Park ♿ Good 💰 Free (except IMAX theatre)

MUSEUM OF TELEVISION AND RADIO

This tribute to more than 70 years of home entertainment investigates aspects of broadcasting from news to *Star Trek* make-up.

➕ Off map, west ✉ 465 N Beverly Drive, Beverly Hills ☎ 310/786 1000 🕐 Wed–Sun noon–5; Thu until 9 🚌 3, 4 ♿ Good 💰 Moderate

MUSEUM OF TOLERANCE

The Simon Wiesenthal Center's thought-provoking museum explores the nature of prejudice (➤ panel for details).

➕ Off map, west ✉ 9786 W Pico Boulevard, West LA ☎ 310/553 8403 🕐 Mon–Thu 10–4; Fri 10–3; Sun 10:30–5 🚌 SM7 ♿ Very good 💰 Moderate

PACIFIC ASIA MUSEUM

Notable Far Eastern art is displayed in rotation alongside visiting exhibitions in an exotic 1920s interpretation of a Chinese imperial palace.

➕ Off map, northeast ✉ 46 N Los Robles Avenue, Pasadena ☎ 818/449 2742 🕐 Wed–Sun 10–5 🚌 401 ♿ Few 💰 Moderate

SOUTHWEST MUSEUM

One of the finest collections of Native American art and artefacts in the country; pity about the somewhat lack-lustre displays.

➕ Off map, north ✉ 234 Museum Drive (Avenue 43 exit off I-110/Pasadena Freeway) ☎ 213/221 2164 🕐 Tue–Sun 11–5 🚌 83 ♿ Few 💰 Moderate

Mona *(Lili Lakich)*, in the Museum of Neon Art

Beit Hashoah (House of the Holocaust)

Opened in 1993, less than a year after the LA riots (➤ 12), the Museum of Tolerance focuses its attentions on both the dynamics of prejudice and racism in America, and the history of the Holocaust. High-tech interactive and experiential exhibits offer a challenging insight into the machinations of bigotry. World War II artefacts and documents on the second floor provide the most moving memorial of all.

TV & MOVIE BUFF STUFF

See Top 25 Sights for
HOLLYWOOD BOULEVARD (► 30)
UNIVERSAL STUDIOS (► 31)

Grave Affair

For years a veiled lady in black brought flowers to Rudolph Valentino's vault at Hollywood Memorial Park Cemetery, 6000 Santa Monica Boulevard, Hollywood, on the anniversary of his death. Others come to visit Cecil B De Mille, Tyrone Power and Douglas Fairbanks. Buster Keaton, Stan Laurel and Bette Davis are among those buried at Forest Lawn Memorial Park, 6300 Forest Lawn Drive. Marilyn Monroe, Natalie Wood and Roy Orbison are at Westwood Memorial Park, 1218 Glendon Avenue.

Forest Lawn Memorial Park

BROADWAY HISTORIC THEATER DISTRICT

For movie fans with an interest in the early days, Downtown Broadway is the place to find the fabulous movie palaces of yesteryear. Several, such as the Los Angeles (No 615), the Palace (No 630), and the Orpheum (► 56), are still open. Guided walk tours are available with the Los Angeles Conservancy (► 19).

🕀 M7–8 ⊠ Broadway, between Third and Ninth Streets 🚇 Pershing Square 🚌 27, 28, 45, 46

CITY OF LOS ANGELES FILM & VIDEO PERMIT OFFICE

If you want to see movie-makers on location, pick up a free copy of the daily shoot sheet from the sixth-floor permit office. It lists every motion picture, television programme, commercial and video being shot in the streets of the city that day.

🕀 D1 ⊠ 6922 Hollywood Boulevard, Hollywood ⏱ Daily 8:30–5 🚌 1

FREDERICK'S OF HOLLYWOOD LINGERIE MUSEUM

This selection of star undergarments displays offerings from Marilyn Monroe, Ingrid Bergman, Zsa Zsa Gabor, Cher, Joan Collins and Belinda Carlisle. Further examples of Frederick's creative way with the female form include a blow-up bra and the cleavage-enhancing Depth Charge.

🕀 D1 ⊠ 6608 Hollywood Boulevard, Hollywood ☎ 213/466 8506 ⏱ Mon–Sat 10–6; Sun noon–5 🚌 1 ♿ None 🎟 Free

GRAVE LINE TOURS

Movie buffs with a taste for the macabre should not miss this two-and-a-half hour orgy of titillating trivia delivered on cue as passengers (known as 'bodies') are chauffeur-driven (in a hearse) past the former homes of the stars and sites of murders, suicides, sexual shenanigans and everyday deviancy in LALALand. (By reservation only.)

➕ D1 ✉ Departs from Orchid Street at Hollywood Boulevard (east side of Mann's Chinese Theater) ☎ 213/469 4149 ⏰ Tue–Sun 9:30
📇 1 ♿ None 💵 Very expensive

HOLLYWOOD ROOSEVELT HOTEL

A romantic rendezvous for Gable and Lombard, where Errol Flynn supposedly invented his own gin cocktail behind the barber shop, and where David Niven slept in the servants' quarters before his star was born, the Roosevelt now presents a historical review of Hollywood from the early days to the 1940s on the second floor.

➕ D1 ✉ 7000 Hollywood Boulevard, Hollywood ☎ 213/466 7000
⏰ Daily 📇 1 ♿ Few 💵 Free

HOLLYWOOD STUDIO MUSEUM

Cecil B De Mille shot Hollywood's first full-length movie in this old horse barn in 1913. Moved from its original site on Vine to the Paramount lot across from the Hollywood Bowl, it now houses collections of film memorabilia and antique movie-making equipment.

➕ D1 ✉ 2100 N Highland Avenue, Hollywood
☎ 213/874 2276 ⏰ Thu–Sun 11–4 📇 1
♿ Few 💵 Inexpensive

MUSEUM OF HOLLYWOOD HISTORY

Following a dramatic facelift, the 1935 former HQ of make-up guru, Max Factor, now houses a new museum and a mountain of movie memorabilia. Trace the history of film make-up from Lon Chaney to *Beetlejuice* and beyond; then step behind the camera for video interviews with top Hollywood directors, cinematographers, special effects supremos, editors and actors.

➕ D1 ✉ 1666 N Highland Avenue, Hollywood
☎ 213/463 6668 ⏰ Daily 10–9 📇 1 ♿ Good 💵 Moderate

WARNER BROTHERS STUDIO VIP TOUR

The best behind-the-scenes tour for the serious movie buff. Small groups (reservations advised; no children under 10) tour backlot sets, watch actual productions in progress where possible, and learn about the nitty-gritty of movie-making.

➕ Off map, northwest ✉ 4000 Warner Boulevard, Burbank
☎ 818/954 1744 ⏰ Mon–Fri 9–4 ♿ Few 📇 96 💵 Very expensive

Lights! Camera! Action!

Dozens of TV shows in search of an audience give away free tickets through agencies such as LIGHTS! CAMERA! ACTION! (☎ 818/509 8497), and Audiences Unlimited (☎ 818/506 0043). You can also apply direct to CBS Studio Center (☎ 818/760 5000) for the likes of *Roseanne*; CBS Television City (☎ 213/852 2624) for *Wheel of Fortune* and *The Price is Right*; NBC Television (☎ 818/840 3537) for *The Tonight Show*; Paramount Studios (☎ 213/956 5575) for *Frasier*; and Warner Bros Studios (☎ 818/954 1744) for *Murphy Brown*.

Charlie Chaplin statue in the Hollywood Roosevelt Hotel

LANDMARKS

Blots on the horizon

Two high-rise districts loom large on the horizon, though they fail to cut much of an architectural dash. At least Downtown can lay claim to the tallest building west of Chicago in the 73-storey First Interstate World Center, 633 W Fifth Street. In West LA, Century City's gleaming towers (access from Avenue of the Stars) make a pretty show of reflecting the sunset in their blank glass faces, but the bland office-shopping-entertainment complex is less than inspiring.

ANGEL'S FLIGHT
From 1901–69 the world's shortest railway ferried passengers up and down Bunker Hill. Newly renovated and returned to service, the historic funicular shuttles between Hill Street and California Plaza like a small black and orange bug.
➕ M7 ✉ Hill Street at Fourth Street ☎ 1–800/266 6883
🕐 Daily 6AM–10PM 💷 Inexpensive

CALIFORNIA PLAZA
Atop Bunker Hill, Downtown's towering concrete and glass financial district, the billion-dollar California Plaza complex houses offices, a hotel and MOCA (▶ 37). Another reason to visit is the mesmerising dancing fountains, animated geysers which bounce and bubble to a multicoloured light show at night.
➕ M7 ✉ Grand Avenue 🚌 DASH B 💷 Free

CAPITOL RECORDS TOWER
Welton Becket's 1954 tower for the company that can list Frank Sinatra and the Beach Boys in its back catalogue is one of Hollywood's most famous landmarks. Though the architect denied it was intentional, it certainly looks like a stack of records topped by a needle.
➕ E1 ✉ 1750 Vine Street, Hollywood 🚌 1

CHIAT/DAY INC ADVERTISING BUILDING
Definitely one for the picture album, the entrance to Frank Gehry's 1985 advertising agency office is flanked by a pair of giant, three-storey-high black binoculars designed by Claes Oldenburg.
➕ Off map, west ✉ 340 Main Street, Venice 🚌 33, 333, SM1

City Hall, Beverly Hills

CITY HALL
This Downtown monolith, the tallest building in the city from 1928 until 1959, still cuts an imposing figure. Once 'destroyed' by Martians in *War of the Worlds*, it is familiar as the *Daily Planet* building in the Superman TV series, the police HQ from *Dragnet*, and has starred in dozens of other TV series and films.
➕ N7 ✉ 200 N Spring Street 🚇 Civic Center 🚌 DASH D

COCA-COLA BOTTLING FACTORY
This 1936 Streamline Moderne triumph by Robert Derrah resembles a giant ocean liner with

riveted port holes for windows, a 'bridge' structure bearing the Coca-Cola logo and a nautical red, white and blue trim.

➕ M10 ✉ 1334 S Central Avenue (at 14th Street) 🚌 53

MANN'S CHINESE THEATER

A Hollywood legend in its own right. Sid Grauman built the Chinese to host extravagant premières in 1927. The oriental hotchpotch of pagoda roofs and twiddly towers, dragon motifs, Fu dogs and temple bells is appealingly kitsch, and there is a splendid art deco interior.

➕ D1 ✉ 6925 Hollywood Boulevard, Hollywood ☎ 213/464 8111 🚌 1

PACIFIC DESIGN CENTER

Beached just off La Cienega Boulevard, this enormous coloured glass leviathan is affectionately known as the 'Blue Whale' for obvious reasons. Actually, there are two buildings by Cesar Pelli and Gruen Associates offering 1.2 million square feet of showroom space.

➕ Off map, west ✉ 8687 Melrose Avenue (w of San Vicente), West Hollywood 🚌 10, 217

TAIL O' THE PUP

Just around the corner from the 'Blue Whale' (above), you can grab a bite to eat and view a famous roadside landmark all at once at this 1946 hotdog-shaped fast food stand.

➕ Off map, west ✉ 329 San Vicente Boulevard (north of Beverly Boulevard, West Hollywood) 🚌 14

WATTS TOWERS

A bizarre beacon in this otherwise run-down neighbourhood, these folk-art towers were built from scrap by Italian immigrant Simon Rodia between 1921 and 1954. Fashioned from steel rods, old bed frames, bottles and more than 10,000 seashells, the central tower is almost 100 feet high. Guided tours recommended.

➕ Off map, south ✉ 1765 E 107th Street, Watts ☎ 213/847 4646

Hollywoodland

The famous Hollywood sign derives from a 1923 promotion when the word 'Hollywoodland' was blazoned across the Hollywood Hills to sell a residential development. The 'land' was knocked off the sign in 1949, and the remaining 50-foot-high letters are probably the city's most recognisable landmark. There are good views from high points all over town, including the Griffith Observatory (➤ 32).

One of the towers at Watts built from scrap

55

HISTORIC BUILDINGS

See Top 25 Sights for
BRADBURY BUILDING (►39)
EL PUEBLO DE LOS ANGELES, AVILA ADOBE
(►41)
GAMBLE HOUSE (►44)
HOLLYHOCK HOUSE (►34)

Mission survivors

Both LA's original Spanish missions still exist in the valleys that took their names. Southeast of Pasadena, the Mission San Gabriel Archangel, 537 W Mission Drive, San Gabriel (☎ 818/457 3035), was founded first in 1771. Although badly shaken by recent earthquakes, it is set in pretty gardens and the church has been reopened. The attractive Mission San Fernando Rey de España, at 15151 San Fernando Mission Boulevard, Mission Hills, appears in better condition, but has been largely reconstructed.

BILTMORE HOTEL

This grand old lady dates from 1923. Enter from Pershing Square to admire the beautifully restored Spanish Revival-style Rendezvous Court lobby.
➕ M7 ✉ 506 S Grand 🚇 Pershing Square 🚌 DASH B, C, E

ENNIS-BROWN HOUSE

The best of Frank Lloyd Wright's Mayan-style concrete structures on a terrific site in the hills near Griffith Park. Privately owned, but occasionally open for tours by reservation.
➕ Off map, northwest ✉ 2655 Glendower Avenue, Los Feliz ☎ 213/660 0607 💷 Expensive

LOS ANGELES CENTRAL LIBRARY

A 1926 Beaux-Arts treasure ornamented with carved reliefs of great thinkers, writers, scientists and choice *bons mots*. Check out the historic 1930s murals in the Cook Rotunda.
➕ M7 ✉ 630 W Fifth Street ☎ 213/228 7000 🕐 Mon, Thu–Sat 10–5:30; Tue–Wed noon–8; Sun 1–5 🚇 Pershing Square 🚌 DASH B, C, E 👍 Good 💷 Free

ORPHEUM THEATRE

Fabulously restored 1911 vaudeville theatre. The original Würlitzer pipe organ is warmed up on Saturday mornings.
➕ M8 ✉ 630 S Broadway ☎ 213/623 2489 🕐 Open for movies; check listings 🚌 27, 28, 45, 46

SCHINDLER HOUSE

Rudolph Schindler's innovative 1921 design for California living. Its indoor/outdoor plan became the prototype for much Southern California vernacular architecture.
➕ Off map, west ✉ 835 N Kings Road, West Hollywood ☎ 213/651 1510 🕐 Wed–Sun 11–6 👍 Few 💷 Moderate

UNION STATION

This Spanish Mission-style beauty was built by the railroad companies in 1939. Take a turn around the main hall to view its lofty, barrel-shaped ceiling and Moorish tile trim.
➕ N6-7 ✉ 800 N Alameda Street 🚇 Union Station 🚌 DASH B, D

Rudolph Schindler's house

GARDENS & GREEN SPACES

DESCANSO GARDENS

Glorious gardens covering 65 acres, including a
30-acre California live oak forest. Spectacular
displays of camellias bloom from January to
March.

🚹 Off map, northeast ✉ 1418 Descanso Drive, La Cañada (Verdugo
Boulevard exit off I-210/Foothill Freeway, northwest of Pasadena)
☎ 818/952 4400 🕐 Daily 9–4:30 except Christmas 🚌 177
🚻 Moderate

EXPOSITION PARK ROSE GARDEN

This fragrant spot boasts around 20,000 rose
bushes from some 200 varieties in a sunken
garden beside the Natural History Museum.

🚹 J11 ✉ Exposition Boulevard 🕐 Open site 🚌 DASH C/Expo
Park 🚻 Free

GREYSTONE PARK

The sloping parklands surrounding oil
millionaire Edward Doheny's vast 1928
Gothic mansion offer fine views.

🚹 Off map, west ✉ 905 Loma Vista Drive, Beverly Hills
☎ 310/550 4654 🕐 Daily 10–5, 6 in summer 🚌 2, 3,
302 🚻 Free

VIRGINIA ROBINSON MANSION & GARDENS

A hidden treasure of Beverly Hills, the
late society hostess Virginia Robinson's
Mediterranean-style villa is set in six
acres of lush gardens and groves with
palms, terraces and water features.

🚹 Off map, west ✉ 1008 Elden Way, Beverly Hills
☎ 310/276 5367 🕐 By reservation only, Tue–Fri
🚻 Moderate

WILL ROGERS STATE HISTORIC PARK

There is plenty of space for the kids to run
wild and picnic on this 186-acre hillside
ranch property. Features include tours of
the Western-style home of the 'Cowboy
Philosopher', a nature trail with great
views, stables and occasional polo games.

🚹 Off map, west ✉ 14253 Sunset Boulevard, Pacific Palisades
☎ 310/454 8212 🕐 Daily 8–5, 7 in summer (house from 10:30)
🚌 2, 302 🚻 Moderate

Touring Eden

A landscape architect and a
landscape designer set up the
guide service Touring Eden
(☎ 818/769 2304) to squire
garden lovers around LA's
horticultural highlights. From
Malibu to Beverly Hills and up to
Pasadena, they offer expert and
enthusiastically guided tours for
individuals and groups (discounts
available). Lunch or tea and
transport from designated pick-up
points is included in the price.

*Virginia Robinson
Gardens*

ATTRACTIONS FOR CHILDREN

Miniature marvels

Wilshire Boulevard's 'Miracle Mile' museums offer an interesting choice of attractions for kids, all within a couple of minutes' walk of each other. The fossils at the George C Page Museum (➤ 50) appeal to little ghouls; the shiny automobiles of the Petersen Automotive Museum (➤ 29) to child racers; and the Carol & Barry Kaye Museum of Miniatures, 5900 Wilshire Boulevard, Midtown (☎ 213/937 MINI), exercises a mesmerising doll's-house charm.

See Top 25 Sights for
AUTRY MUSEUM OF WESTERN HERITAGE (➤ 33)
DISNEYLAND (➤ 48)
GRIFFITH PARK (➤ 32)
NATURAL HISTORY MUSEUM OF LOS ANGELES COUNTY (➤ 35)
RANCHO LOS ALAMITOS (➤ 43)
UNIVERSAL STUDIOS (➤ 31)

HOLLYWOOD GUINNESS WORLD OF RECORDS MUSEUM

Trivia galore from The-Animal-with-The-Smallest-Brain-in-Proportion-to-Body-Size (a *Stegosaurus*) to the Most Biographed Female (Marilyn Monroe).

✚ D1 ⊠ 6764 Hollywood Boulevard, Hollywood ☎ 213/463 6433 🕐 Daily 10–midnight 🚇 1 💷 Moderate

KNOTT'S BERRY FARM

The nation's first theme park. Visit Camp Snoopy and the 1880s frontier Ghost Town; splash down in Wild Water Wilderness and ride the Jaguar roller-coaster; or watch a crafts demonstration in the Indian Trails area.

✚ Off map, southeast ⊠ 8039 Beach Boulevard, Buena Park ☎ 714/220 5200 🕐 Summer, daily 9–midnight; winter, Mon–Fri 10–6; Sat 10–10; Sun 10–7 🚌 460 💷 Very expensive

MUSEUM OF FLYING

The history of flight, vintage planes, video kiosks and interactive exhibits plus antique planes in the skies some weekends.

✚ Off map, southwest ⊠ 2772 N Donald Douglas Loop, Santa Monica Airport ☎ 310/392 8822 🕐 Tue–Sun 10–5 🚌 SM8 💷 Moderate

PACIFIC PARK

A seaside fairground with rides, side-shows and amusement arcades opened on Santa Monica Pier in 1996.

✚ Off map, west ⊠ Santa Monica Pier, opposite Colorado Avenue ☎ 310/260 8744 🕐 Seasonal schedules 🚌 20, 22, 33, SM1, 7, 10 💷 Free access to Pier

Shopfront detail, Hollywood Boulevard

SIX FLAGS CALIFORNIA

San Fernando Valley's theme park duo: Magic Mountain, renowned for its hair-raising thrill rides; and the new Hurricane Harbor Water Park.

✚ Off map, northwest ⊠ Magic Mountain exit off I–5/Golden State Freeway ☎ 818/367 5965 🕐 Call for schedules 🚆 Metrolink to Santa Clarita, then SCT30 💷 Very expensive

FREE ATTRACTIONS

*Santa Monica beach
and pier*

CABRILLO AQUARIUM

Dozens of aquariums and displays explore
Southern Californian marine life from the fantail
sole known for its camouflage abilities to the
bizarre grunnion, a fish that comes ashore to breed.

⊞ Off map, south ⊠ Stephen White Drive (off Pacific Avenue), San
Pedro ☎ 310/548 7562 ⏰ Tue–Fri noon–5; Sat–Sun 10–5 🚌 446

FRANKLIN D MURPHY SCULPTURE GARDEN

Sculptures by such artists as Arp, Hepworth and
Calder are sprinkled liberally over sunny lawns
shaded by jacaranda trees. Henry Moore, Miró,
Maillol and Rodin feature on the tree-lined
promenade.

⊞ Off map, west ⊠ UCLA Campus off Circle Drive East, Westwood
⏰ Open site 🚌 2, 302, SM1, 2, 3, 8, 12 (off Sunset Boulevard)

MULHOLLAND DRIVE

This winding mountain road with terrific views
runs from Hollywood west past Malibu (with an
unpaved section through Topanga State Park).
Access to the eastern section off Laurel Canyon
Boulevard; to the western section from Old
Topanga Canyon Road.

Take a tour

The West Coast's biggest
newspaper, the *Los Angeles Times*,
offers free behind-the-scenes
tours of its offices on weekdays
(☎ 213/237 5757); and there
are free tours of the attractively
landscaped UCLA campus at
Westwood (☎ 310/825 8764).
On Pasadena's 'Millionaires' Row',
the Wrigley Gardens at
Tournament House, 391 S Orange
Grove Boulevard (☎ 818/449
4100), are open daily with free
tours on Thursday afternoons
from February to August.

BEACHES

See Top 25 Sights for
SANTA MONICA AND VENICE BEACH (▶ 24)
LONG BEACH AND THE *QUEEN MARY* (▶ 42)

Hermosa Beach

HERMOSA BEACH
Slipped in between the other two major South Bay beaches, Manhattan and Redondo, Hermosa is renowned as LA's leading party beach. Lots of hanging out and volleyball for the well-toned.
🚩 Off map, southwest ✉ Off Pacific Coast Highway, Hermosa Beach 🚌 439

LEO CARRILLO STATE BEACH
On the LA County line beyond Malibu. Broad, mile-long sandy beach divided by Sequit Point. Surfing to the north; tide pools to entertain the kids; and underwater caves revealed at low tide.
🚩 Off map, west ✉ Off Pacific Coast Highway (11 miles west of Malibu) 🚌 434

MALIBU SURFRIDER STATE BEACH
One of California's original surfing beaches, 'The Bu' offers the best waves during the late-summer southern swells (Aug–Sep).
🚩 Off map, west ✉ Off Pacific Coast Highway, Malibu 🚌 434

MANHATTAN BEACH
Fashionable beach suburb with cafés along the seafront. Good swimming, surfing and games.
🚩 Off map, southwest ✉ Manhattan Beach Boulevard (off Pacific Coast Highway), Manhattan Beach 🚌 439

Off-the-beaten track
It is no easy task to escape the crowds. However, there are a few relatively quiet corners, namely a handful of small coves tucked into the steep, rocky bluffs of the Palos Verdes peninsula. On the north side, beyond Redondo Beach, try sandy Malaga Cove. Around to the south, near Lloyd Wright's Wayfarer's Chapel, Abalone Cove's rock pools provide entertainment and there is good snorkelling.

REDONDO BEACH
Hotel-lined beach with good swimming and a heated lagoon for children. Fishing from the pier.
🚩 Off map, southwest ✉ Off Pacific Coast Highway, Redondo Beach 🚌 439

WILL ROGERS STATE BEACH
Just north of Santa Monica, this is a good family beach with parking and fewer crowds.
🚩 Off map, west ✉ Off Pacific Coast Highway (opposite Sunset Boulevard), Pacific Palisades 🚌 434

ZUMA BEACH
LA's biggest beach and a hot favourite with the legendary Valley (San Fernando) Girls (and boys). Hip, action-packed and crowded on weekends.
🚩 Off map, west ✉ Off Pacific Coast Highway (6 miles west of Malibu) 🚌 434

LOS ANGELES
where to...

EXPENSIVE RESTAURANTS

Prices

Average meal per head
excluding drinks
£ = up to $15
££ = $15 to $30
£££ = over $30

Except for the luxury restaurants on this page, where dinner will easily cost upwards of $70 for two people excluding wine (lunch will be less; typically around $40), dining in Los Angeles need not cost an arm and a leg. If you eat in reasonable restaurants, anticipate spending around $6–8 per person for breakfast, $10 for lunch, and $15–20 for dinner excluding drinks. Wherever you dine, a tip of at least 15 per cent of the bill excluding wine is expected.

Opening times

All the listed restaurants are open daily for lunch and dinner unless otherwise stated. Angelenos generally lunch between 11:30–2, and dine between 6–9, though many restaurants open earlier and/or close later than these times.

ARNIE MORTON'S OF CHICAGO (£££)
Clubby atmosphere and superlative steaks, plus lobster, swordfish and salmon.
➕ Off map, west ✉ 435 S La Cienega, Beverly Hills ☎ 310/246 1501 ⦿ Dinner only 🚌 2, 3, 16, 105

BERNARD'S (£££)
Lovely restaurant in the historic Biltmore Hotel. Seafood is a speciality, and harp music in the evening makes this a favourite romantic spot.
➕ M7 ✉ Biltmore Hotel, 506 S Grand Avenue ☎ 213/612 1580 🚇 Pershing Square 🚌 DASH B, C, E

THE DINING ROOM (£££)
Beautiful formal dining room serving elegant Continental/American cuisine. Lengthy wine list; polished service.
➕ Off map, west ✉ Regent Beverly Wilshire Hotel, 9500 Wilshire Boulevard, Beverly Hills ☎ 310/274 8179 🚌 20, 21, 22

FENIX (£££)
Stunning art deco dining room with views and inventive California/French menu. Noted wine cellar.
➕ Off map, west ✉ Argyle Hotel, 8358 Sunset Boulevard, West Hollywood ☎ 213/848 6677 ⦿ Closed Sun dinner (bar menu available) 🚌 2, 3

MORTON'S (£££)
Stylish film-industry favourite packed with celebs grazing from the slightly health-conscious American menu.
➕ Off map, west ✉ 8764 Melrose Avenue, West Hollywood ☎ 310/276 5205 ⦿ Closed Sat lunch and Sun 🚌 10

L'ORANGERIE (£££)
Ineffably grand French restaurant with palatial décor, impeccable service and a modern-classic menu. Terrace dining.
➕ Off map, west ✉ 903 N La Cienega Boulevard, West Hollywood ☎ 310/652 9770 ⦿ Closed Mon, dinner only 🚌 4, 105

PATINA (£££)
Exceptional modern French cuisine in a relaxed setting. Chef Joachim Splichal is probably the brightest star in LA's culinary firmament.
➕ E3 ✉ 5955 Melrose Avenue, Hollywood ☎ 213/467 1108 ⦿ Closed Mon lunch 🚌 10

REX IL RISTORANTE (£££)
Glamorous art deco setting complete with Lalique fixtures and the best Italian food in the city. Risottos to rave about.
➕ M7 ✉ 617 S Olive Street ☎ 213/627 2300 ⦿ Lunch Thu–Fri, dinner Mon–Sat; closed Sun 🚇 Pershing Square 🚌 DASH B, C, E

SPAGO (£££)
Chef Wolfgang Puck's celebrity-studded haunt. Fine Californian cuisine including the famous (but pricey) designer pizza.
➕ Off map, west ✉ 1174 Horn Avenue, West Hollywood ☎ 310/652 4025 ⦿ Dinner only 🚌 2, 3

BUDGET RESTAURANTS

BELMONT BREWING COMPANY (£)

Home-brewed beer and casual American menu. Dine out on the beachfront terrace.

⊞ Off map, south ✉ 25 39th Place, Long Beach ☎ 310/433 3891 🚌 LBT 121

CANTER'S (£)

Classic Fairfax District deli serving kosher specials, huge pastrami sandwiches and waitress banter 24 hours a day.

⊞ B4 ✉ 419 N Fairfax Avenue, Midtown ☎ 213/651 2030 🚌 14, 217

DIVE! (£)

Steven Spielberg has a hand in this submarine-themed spot, an upscale sandwich shop. Huge hit with kids.

⊞ Off map, west ✉ Century City Shopping Center, 10250 Santa Monica Boulevard, West LA ☎ 310/788 3483 🚌 4, 22, 322

KOKOMO (£)

Freshly baked muffins, deli sandwiches, steaming bowls of tasty gumbo, salads – all good reasons to brave the Farmers' Market.

⊞ B4 ✉ Farmers' Market, 6333 W Third Street, Midtown ☎ 213/933 0773 🚌 16, 217

MANDARIN DELI (£)

Chinese *dim sum* (dumplings) and noodle dishes every which way.

⊞ N6 ✉ 727 N Broadway ☎ 213/623 6054 🚌 DASH B

NATE 'N' AL (£)

Vinyl banquettes in Beverly Hills? Yes, at this famous deli with occasional celebrity diners.

⊞ Off map, west ✉ 414 N Beverly Drive, Beverly Hills ☎ 310/274 0101 🚌 4

PASADENA BAKING COMPANY (£)

Great bakery in the Old Town. Muffins, croissants, pastries, sandwiches and coffee on the terrace until late.

⊞ Off map, northeast ✉ 29 E Colorado Boulevard, Pasadena ☎ 818/796 9966 🚌 401

PHILIPPE THE ORIGINAL (£)

Crusty fried bread French dip sandwiches piled high with meats, cheese and extra hot mustard. Heroic breakfasts, home-made pies.

⊞ N6 ✉ 1001 N Alameda Street ☎ 213/628 3781 🚇 Union Station 🚌 DASH B

PINK'S FAMOUS CHILI DOGS (£)

This take-away stand is an LA institution. Foot-long jalepeño dogs, burgers and tamales until 2AM.

⊞ C3 ✉ 6919 Melrose Avenue, Midtown ☎ 213/931 4223 🚌 10

TONY'S FAMOUS FRENCH DIP SANDWICHES (£)

Hunger-demolishing French dip sandwiches, soups and salads in the Downtown district.

⊞ Off map, south ✉ 701 Long Beach Boulevard, Long Beach ☎ 310/435 6238 🚇 Metro Blue Line/Pacific Avenue 🚌 LBT 41, 42, 43, 44

Malls and markets

LA's numerous shopping malls, such as the Beverly Center (➤ 71) and Downtown's Seventh Street Marketplace (➤ 71), are a good source of cheap eats offering a wide choice of fast-food outlets as well as delis and ethnic take-away counters with shared seating. The touristy-tacky Farmers' Market (➤ 71) has a wide choice of budget eateries, particularly popular at the weekend, while the down-to-earth Grand Central Market (➤ 38) is the best place to find budget bites Downtown bar none.

AMERICAN RESTAURANTS

Eating with children

LA's plethora of chic dining haunts is not particularly child friendly, but fortunately there are plenty of other options. Family restaurants and burger chains abound, particularly near Disneyland and around the South Bay beach area. Always check if the restaurant has a children's menu for smaller portions and lower prices, and as a special treat all children love perching at the bar to slurp on a milkshake at one of the 1950s-style themed diners.

ED DEBEVIC'S (££)
1950s theme diner with the requisite retro styling, wacky waitresses, burgers, chilli and calorific pies.
⊞ Off map, west ✉ 134 N La Cienega Boulevard, Beverly Hills ☎ 310/659 1952 🚌 20, 21, 22, 105

ENGINE CO NO 28 (££)
Handsome bar and grill in a converted 1912 fire station. Steaks, seafood, spicy French fries and good wine list.
⊞ L7 ✉ 644 S Figueroa Street ☎ 213/624 6996 🕐 Closed lunch at weekends 🚇 7th Street/Metro Center 🚌 DASH A, B

GREENBLATT'S (£)
A haven for homesick New Yorkers, Greenblatt's dishes up quality deli favourites from corn beef to cheesecake.
⊞ B2 ✉ 8017 Sunset Boulevard, West Hollywood ☎ 213/656 0606 🚌 2

HARD ROCK CAFÉ (££)
Loud music, rock memorabilia and decent hamburgers – the queues go on, and on, and on.
⊞ Off map, west ✉ Beverly Center, Beverly Boulevard (at La Cienega), West Hollywood ☎ 310/276 7605 🚌 10, 14, 105, 217

JOHNNY ROCKET'S (£)
One of a popular chain of *American Graffiti*-era diners.
⊞ Off map, west ✉ 474 N Beverly Drive, Beverly Hills ☎ 310/271 2222 🚌 4

LAWRY'S THE PRIME RIB (£££)
Aged prime rib, Yorkshire pudding, creamed spinach and horseradish sauce. Clubby surroundings; established 1938.
⊞ Off map, west ✉ 100 N La Cienega Boulevard, Beverly Hills ☎ 310/652 2827 🕐 Dinner only 🚌 20, 21, 22, 105

MUSSO & FRANK GRILL (££-£££)
A dim, wood-panelled Hollywood institution where deals are struck over dry martinis and steaks and chops.
⊞ D2 ✉ 6667 Hollywood Boulevard, Hollywood ☎ 213/467 7788 🕐 Closed Sun–Mon 🚌 1

PLANET HOLLYWOOD (£-££)
The Stallone-Willis-Schwarzenegger place serving up movie memorabilia, 'all-American' hamburgers, pizzas and salads.
⊞ Off map, west ✉ 9560 Wilshire Boulevard, Beverly Hills ☎ 310/275 7828 🚌 20, 21, 22

THE RAYMOND (£££)
Pretty, historic California bungalow with garden patios and mixed menu of salads, entrées and home-made desserts.
⊞ Off map, northeast ✉ 1250 S Fair Oaks Avenue, Pasadena ☎ 818/441 3136 🕐 Closed Mon 🚌 483

THUNDER ROADHOUSE (££)
Meatloaf, chilli, burgers and beer-guzzling in a Harley Davidson shop-cum-restaurant-bar.
⊞ Off map, west ✉ 8371 Sunset Boulevard, West Hollywood ☎ 213/650 6011 🚌 2, 3

CALIFORNIAN & PACIFIC RIM RESTAURANTS

CALIFORNIA PIZZA KITCHEN (££)

Pizza the California designer way, plus huge salads, well-stuffed calzones and a buzzy, lively atmosphere. At several locations.

➕ Off map, west ✉ 121 N La Cienega Boulevard, Beverly Hills ☎ 310/854 6555 🚌 14, 16, 105

CHAYA BRASSERIE (£££)

Minimalist décor with a Japanese influence that's also evident in the innovative and intriguing East-meets-West menu. Also Chaya Venice at the beach.

➕ Off map, west ✉ 8741 Alden Drive, West Hollywood ☎ 310/859 8833 🕐 Dinner only at weekends 🚌 14, 16

CHINOIS ON MAIN STREET (£££)

Another bustling and stylish showcase for chef Wolfgang Puck's sensational California-Chinese creations.

➕ Off map, west ✉ 2709 Main Street, Santa Monica ☎ 310/392 9025 🕐 Closed for lunch Sat–Tue 🚌 33, SM1

THE IVY (£££)

Reservations are a must for this film-folk hang-out. Great food and terrace dining.

➕ Off map, west ✉ 113 N Robertson Boulevard, West Hollywood ☎ 310/274 8303 🚌 14, 16

MICHAEL'S (£££)

A California culinary pioneer, with an impressive contemporary art collection and lovely terrace.

➕ Off map, west ✉ 1147 Third Street, Santa Monica ☎ 310/451 0843 🕐 Closed Sun–Mon, and Sat lunch 🚌 20, 33, SM2

NICOLA (£££)

A striking futuristic setting for chef Larry Nicola's California-Asian menu.

➕ L7 ✉ 601 S Figueroa Street ☎ 213/485 0927 🕐 Closed Sat lunch and Sun 🚇 7th Street/Metro Center 🚌 DASH A, B

PANGAEA (£££)

Sophisticated and creative Pacific Rim cuisine. Excellent seafood.

➕ Off map, west ✉ Hotel Nikko at Beverly Hills, 465 S La Cienega Boulevard ☎ 310/246 2100 🚌 20, 21, 22

PARKWAY GRILL (£££)

Cutting-edge California fare with Southwestern accents.

➕ Off map, northeast ✉ 510 S Arroyo Parkway, Pasadena ☎ 818/795 1001 🕐 Closed Sat lunch 🚌 401, 402

ROCKENWAGNER (££)

European ambience and beautifully prepared dishes using the freshest local ingredients.

➕ Off map, west ✉ 2435 Main Street, Santa Monica ☎ 310/399 6504 🕐 Closed Mon lunch 🚌 33, SM1

WOLFGANG PUCK CAFÉ (£)

Sample abbreviated versions of the master's California-Asian fusion fare. Also Santa Monica and Universal City.

➕ B2 ✉ 8000 Sunset Boulevard, West Hollywood ☎ 213/650 7300 🚌 2, 3

California drinking

California wines make a fine accompaniment to almost any meal. Most come from the 400 or so wineries located in the Napa and Sonoma valleys north of San Francisco, where common grape varieties include Cabernet Sauvignon and Chardonnay, as well as California's unique varietal, Zinfandel, used to produce red, white and pink wines. Winemakers' names to look out for include Beringer, Charles Krug, Christian Brothers, Inglenook, Lytton Springs, Ridge, Stag's Leap, and also *méthode champenoise* sparkling wines from Domaine Chandon.

MEXICAN & SOUTHWESTERN RESTAURANTS

A-maizing

Ground maize (or sweetcorn flour) is a Mexican staple, and the chief ingredient of *tortillas*, the ubiquitous cornmeal pancakes that turn up in any number of guises on Mexican menus. Some of the most common varieties are soft, folded *burritos*, stuffed and deep-fried enchiladas, crescent-shaped, deep-fried *quesadillas* filled with cheese and chillies (a useful vegetarian option), and crispy folded *tacos* (*taco* literally means 'snack' in Mexican).

ABIQUIU (£££)

Delectable Southwestern cuisine created with a light but assured (and occasionally fiery) touch. Patio dining.

⊞ Off map, west ✉ 1413 Fifth Street, Santa Monica ☎ 310/395 8611 ⊙ Closed for lunch at weekends ▣ 4, SM1, 7, 10

BARNEY'S BEANERY (£–££)

Generous portions of Tex-Mex fare and hamburgers plus a lengthy beer menu in friendly roadhouse-style diner with bar and pool table.

⊞ Off map, west ✉ 8447 Santa Monica Boulevard, West Hollywood ☎ 213/654 2287 ▣ 4

BORDER GRILL (££)

Always packed with a loud, eclectic crowd. Great Mexican food with an inventive twist.

⊞ Off map, west ✉ 1445 Fourth Street, Santa Monica ☎ 310/451 1655 ⊙ Dinner only ▣ 4, SM1, 7, 10

EL CHOLO (££)

LA institution (established 1927) serving Mexican fare in hacienda-style surroundings with patio tables.

⊞ Off map, west ✉ 1121 S Western Avenue, Midtown ☎ 213/734 2773 ▣ 30, 31

EL TORITO GRILL (££)

Busy, fun place offering a wide range of Mexican and Southwestern dishes washed down with tequila.

⊞ Off map, west ✉ 9595 Wilshire Boulevard, Beverly Hills ☎ 310/550 1599 ⊙ Daily; closed Thanksgiving, Christmas ▣ 20, 21, 22

LA GOLONDRINA (££)

Classic Mexican joint in El Pueblo. *Mariachi* musicians and *margaritas* on tap.

⊞ N6 ✉ W-17 Olvera Street ☎ 213/628 4349 🚇 Union Station ▣ DASH B

MATRIX TEX-MEX PLAYA (£–££)

Beachfront Tex-Mex cantina at Pacific Palisades with cheery *margarita*-fuelled atmosphere.

⊞ Off map, west ✉ 118 Entrada Drive, Santa Monica ☎ 310/459 8596 ▣ 434

MERIDA (£)

Small and friendly local Mexican restaurant serving Yucatan specialities. Patio dining.

⊞ Off map, northeast ✉ 20 E Colorado Boulevard, Pasadena ☎ 818/792 7371 ▣ 483

REBECCA'S (£££)

Designer décor (Frank Gehry and suspended metal crocodiles) plus equally fashionable Mexican-inspired menu.

⊞ Off map, west ✉ 2025 Pacific Avenue, Venice Beach ☎ 310/306 6266 ⊙ Dinner only ▣ 33

SONORA CAFÉ (£££)

Southwestern cuisine and suitably tasteful home-on-the-range décor. Historic *margaritas*.

⊞ Off map, west ✉ 180 S La Brea Avenue, Midtown ☎ 213/857 1800 ⊙ Closed Sat, Sun lunch ▣ 14

ASIAN RESTAURANTS

CHAN DARA (£–££)

Small, trendy and popular Thai dining room. Spicy soups and curries, satay and good noodles.

🔲 Off map, west ✉ 1511 N Cahuenga Boulevard, Hollywood ☎ 213/464 8585 🚌 2, 3

HAMA SUSHI (££)

Bustling *sushi* bar where the skilled chefs' flashing blades provide a riveting spectacle.

🔲 N7 ✉ Japanese Village Plaza Mall (off E Second Street), Little Tokyo ☎ 213/680 3454 🄯 Closed Sun lunch 🚌 DASH A

HORIKAWA (£££)

Up-scale and traditional Japanese businessmen's haunt. *Sushi*, *teppanyaki* grill and private dining rooms.

🔲 N7 ✉ 111 San Pedro Street, Little Tokyo ☎ 213/680 9355 🄯 Closed Sat lunch and Sun 🚌 DASH A

JOSS (££)

Sleek Chinese restaurant serving several unusual specialities such as Mongolian lamb.

🔲 Off map, west ✉ 9255 Sunset Boulevard, Hollywood ☎ 310/276 1886 🄯 Closed lunch at weekends 🚌 2, 3

KATSU (£££)

Top-rated *sushi* bar. The freshest and best ingredients served amidst minimalist décor.

🔲 Off map, northwest ✉ 1972 N Hillhurst Avenue, Los Feliz ☎ 213/665 1891 🄯 Closed for lunch on weekends 🚌 26, 204

MON KEE (££–£££)

Seafood is the speciality at this Chinatown favourite. Expect long waits, but great food.

🔲 N6 ✉ 679 N Spring Street ☎ 213/628 6717 🚌 DASH B

OCEAN SEAFOOD (££)

Vast Cantonese restaurant serving affordable fresh seafood dishes, plus *dim sum* and other favourites.

🔲 N6 ✉ 747 N Broadway ☎ 213/687 3088 🚌 DASH B

TALESAI (££)

Up-scale and attractive Thai restaurant with some unusual specialities from salmon to veal.

🔲 Off map, west ✉ 9043 Sunset Boulevard, West Hollywood ☎ 310/275 9724 🄯 Closed Sat lunch and Sun 🚌 2, 3

THOUSAND CRANES (£££)

Fine Japanese cuisine, *sushi* and *tempura* counters, charming service and views over a Japanese garden.

🔲 N7 ✉ New Otani Hotel, 120 S Los Angeles Street, Little Tokyo ☎ 213/629 1200 🄯 Closed Sat lunch 🚌 DASH A

WOO LAE OAK OF SEOUL (££)

Modern Korean cooking has finally made it out of Koreatown and attracts adventurous diners.

🔲 Off map, west ✉ 170 N La Cienega Boulevard, Beverly Hills ☎ 310/652 4187 🚌 20, 21, 22, 105

Snack stops

Dim sum (Chinese dumplings) or noodle dishes make a great and inexpensive lunchtime treat. A short snack can turn into a veritable feast at such notable *dim sum* parlours as Chinatown's Mandarin Deli, 727 N Broadway, or Grandview Gardens, 944 N Hill Street. For an affordable *sushi* blow-out, make tracks for the all-you-can-eat *sushi* counter at Lighthouse Buffet, 201 Arizona Avenue, Santa Monica.

CAFÉS & COFFEE SHOPS

CROCODILE CAFÉ (£)
One of a fast-growing chain of informal, California cuisine cafés specialising in gourmet pizzas, pasta and salads.
✚ Off map, west ✉ 101 Santa Monica Boulevard, Santa Monica ☎ 310/394 4783 🚍 21, 22, 33, SM1, 7, 10

DUKE'S (£)
No frills coffee shop and entertainment industry hang-out. Nothing over $10.
✚ Off map, west ✉ 8909 Sunset Boulevard, West Hollywood ☎ 310/652 3100 🚍 2, 3

GOOD STUFF (£)
South Bay health food outpost with ocean views and a loyal clientele of lycra-clad roller-bladers.
✚ Off map, southwest ✉ 1286 The Strand, Hermosa Beach ☎ 310/374 2334 🚍 439

MARKET CITY CAFFE (££)
Bustling Italian café offering tempting antipasto treats, pasta, salads, home-made bread.
✚ Off map, northeast ✉ 33 S Fair Oaks Avenue, Pasadena ☎ 818/568 0203 🚍 180, 181, 483

POW WOW ESPRESSO BAR (£)
A handy stop on Sunset serving gourmet coffees, croissants, sandwiches, pastries and desserts.
✚ Off map, west ✉ 8868 Sunset Boulevard, West Hollywood ☎ 310/854 0668 🚍 2, 3

SHENANDOAH CAFÉ (££)
Southern specialities include Louisiana-style gumbo and Texas beef briskets.
✚ Off map, southeast ✉ 4722 E 2nd Street, Belmont Shore (Long Beach) ☎ 310/434 3469 🚍 LBT 131

SIDEWALK CAFÉ (£)
Great people-watching from the beachfront terrace. Sandwiches, salads, tostadas, burgers.
✚ Off map, west ✉ 1401 Ocean Front Walk, Venice Beach ☎ 310/399 5547 🚍 33

THE SOURCE (£)
Long-standing vegetarian and vegan landmark on 'The Strip'.
✚ Off map, west ✉ 8301 Sunset Boulevard, West Hollywood ☎ 213/656 6388 🚍 2, 3

VILLAGE COFFEE SHOP (£)
Laid-back, friendly haunt of creative types in the Hollywood Hills serving good, home-cooked food.
✚ Off map, northwest ✉ 2695 Beachwood Drive, Hollywood ☎ 213/467 5398 ⊙ Closed Sun 🚍 208

WORLD CAFÉ (£-££)
Busy restaurant/bar with a good line in wood-fired pizzas, pastas and vegetarian dishes.
✚ Off map, west ✉ 2820 Main Street, Santa Monica ☎ 310/392 1661 🚍 33, SM1

Sunday brunch
Each week when Sunday rolls around, Angelenos gear up to 'do' brunch. Generally served from around 10 or 11 until 2, numerous restaurants throughout the city lay on a variation of the combination breakfast and lunch theme with a set-price menu. However, the most popular brunch spots tend to be found on the coast, and patio dining is at a premium.

MISCELLANEOUS SELECTION (FISHY & FUNKY)

BOOK SOUP BISTRO (£)
Literary types gather for book signings and readings, grilled vegetable soup, salads and atmosphere.
✚ Off map, west ✉ 8800 Sunset Boulevard, West Hollywood ☎ 310/657 1072 🚌 2, 3

CHEESECAKE FACTORY (£–££)
A Mecca for dessert-lovers. Diet-defying portions of cheesecake • in more than 30 different guises.
✚ Off map, west ✉ 364 N Beverly Drive, Beverly Hills ☎ 310/278 7270 🚌 20, 21, 22

DC3 (££)
Californian cuisine for plane-spotters. Fresh pasta, grilled seafood and uninterrupted runway views.
✚ Off map, southwest ✉ 2800 Donald Douglas Loop North, Santa Monica Airport ☎ 310/399 2323 🕐 Closed Mon dinner, Fri dinner and Sat 🚌 SM8

FIG TREE (££)
Enjoy fresh grilled fish and vegetarian dishes served up on a quiet, sunny patio close to the beach.
✚ Off map, west ✉ 429 Ocean Front Walk, Venice Beach ☎ 310/392 4937 🚌 33

GORDON BIERSCH BREWERY (££)
Alfresco dining and people-watching, beers from the in-house micro-brewery and good California cuisine.
✚ Off map, northeast ✉ 41 Hugus Alley, Old Town Pasadena ☎ 818/449 0052 🚌 177

INN OF THE 7TH RAY (££)
Laid-back New Age hangout in lovely setting. Vegetarian and wholefood menu plus special barbecued chicken.
✚ Off map, west ✉ 128 Old Topanga Road, Malibu ☎ 310/455 1311

MCCORMICK & SCHMICK'S (££)
Downtown outpost of a popular chain of attractive, traditional-style fish restaurants. Also in Beverly Hills' Via Rodeo complex.
✚ L7 ✉ First Interstate World Center, 633 W Fifth Street (4th floor) ☎ 213/629 1929 🕐 Closed lunch at weekends 🚌 DASH B, C, D

SADDLE PEAK LODGE (£££)
Rustic and romantic hunting lodge hideaway in the Santa Monica Mountains. Excellent game dishes in season.
✚ Off map, northwest ✉ 419 Cold Canyon Road, Calabasas (San Fernando Valley) ☎ 310/456 7325 🕐 Dinner Wed–Sun and Sun brunch

STINKING ROSE (££)
Garlic-laden Italian and California specialities.
✚ Off map, west ✉ 55 N La Cienega, Beverly Hills ☎ 310/NLA-ROSE 🕐 Dinner only 🚌 20, 21, 22, 105

WATER GRILL (££)
Renowned seafood restaurant with oyster bar and underwater-themed mural.
✚ M7 ✉ 544 S Grand Avenue, Downtown ☎ 213/891 0900 🕐 Daily; closed Sat–Sun lunch 🚌 DASH B, E

Celebrity hosts
The latest craze among Hollywood folk is owning your own restaurant. While Sly, Bruce and Arnie conquer the world with Planet Hollywood (➤ 64); Easy Riders Peter Fonda and Dennis Hopper are long-time partners in Thunder Roadhouse (➤ 64); Steven Spielberg and Jerry Katzenberg are riding high with DIVE! (➤ 63); Dan Ackroyd has a finger in the pie at The House of Blues (➤ 79); and Arnie crops up again with wife, Maria Shriver, at Schatzi on Main in Santa Monica.

SHOPPING DISTRICTS

The Garment District

Downtown's Garment District is for bargain hunters. Centred around Los Angeles Street (between 8th and 11th Streets), dozens of discount retail, jobber and manufacturers' outlet stores offer fashion buys at bargain prices. Check out the Cooper Building, one of Southern California's largest outlet and discount fashion centres at 860 Los Angeles Street, with more than 50 stores spread over six floors.

MAIN STREET

Hip boutiques, arty design and novelty shops helpfully interspersed with good restaurants.

🚩 Off map, west ✉ Main Street (between Hollister and Rose Avenues), Santa Monica 🚌 SM1

MELROSE AVENUE

A three-mile strip of the esoteric and exotic from cutting-edge fashion and retro boutiques to galleries and gift stores. Riveting window-shopping, dining and entertainment.

🚩 D3 ✉ Melrose Avenue (between Highland Avenue and Doheny Drive), Hollywood 🚌 10

MONTANA AVENUE

Ten blocks of super up-scale shopping for the woman with almost everything. Designer boutiques, elegant home-decorating emporiums and luxurious beauty salons.

🚩 Off map, west ✉ Montana Avenue (between Seventh and 17th Streets), Santa Monica 🚌 SM3

OLD TOWN PASADENA

Bisected by Colorado Boulevard, this restored 12-square block enclave offers an appealing selection of boutiques, galleries, gift stores and eateries.

🚩 Off map, northeast ✉ Colorado Boulevard (between Arroyo Parkway and Delacey Avenue), Pasadena 🚌 177, 180, 181, 401, 402, 483, 485

RODEO DRIVE

LA's answer to London's Bond Street and Rome's Via Condotti, Rodeo Drive is a gold-plated shopping experience. Top designer clothes and accessories, a surfeit of jewellers and chic retail complexes.

🚩 Off map, west ✉ Rodeo Drive, Beverly Hills 🚌 4, 20, 21, 22

SUNSET PLAZA

An exclusive little cluster of ultra-fashionable boutiques and sidewalk bistros on 'The Strip'.

🚩 Off map, west ✉ Sunset Boulevard (between San Vicente and La Cienega Boulevards), West Hollywood 🚌 2, 3

THIRD STREET PROMENADE

Shoppers, buskers and street vendors jostle along the pedestrianised Promenade with its wide selection of shopping, dining and entertainment options.

🚩 Off map, west ✉ Third Street (between Wilshire Boulevard and Broadway), Santa Monica 🚌 20, 22, SM1, 2, 7, 8, 9, 10

WESTWOOD VILLAGE

Outdoor cafés add to the appeal of this European-style 'Village' offering fashion, sports and music stores designed to appeal to well-scrubbed UCLA students from the neighbouring campus.

🚩 Off map, west ✉ Westwood Boulevard (off Wilshire Boulevard), Westwood 🚌 20, 21, 22, SM1, 2, 3, 8, 12

SHOPPING CENTRES & MALLS

BEVERLY CENTER
Major league up-scale mall with more than 160 fashion, department and speciality stores, cinemas and restaurants.
➕ Off map, west ✉ 8500 Beverly Boulevard, West Hollywood ☎ 310/854 0070
🚌 14, 16, 105, 202

CENTURY CITY SHOPPING CENTER & MARKETPLACE
Some 140 stores crammed into LA's premier outdoor shopping, dining and entertainment complex.
➕ Off map, west ✉ 10250 Santa Monica Boulevard, West LA ☎ 310/553 5300 🚌 4, 22, 322

DEL AMO FASHION CENTER
Humongous South Bay retail centre anchored by half-a-dozen department stores including Sears.
➕ Off map, southwest ✉ Hawthorne Boulevard (at Carson), Torrance ☎ 310/542 8525

GLENDALE GALLERIA
Giant San Gabriel Valley mall featuring The Broadway, Nordstrom's, and JC Penney with some 250 other stores and restaurants.
➕ Off map, north ✉ 2148 Glendale Galleria, Glendale ☎ 818/240 9481 🚌 180, 181

LONG BEACH PLAZA
Shopping and dining in the heart of Downtown Long Beach. JC Penney, Montgomery Ward, plus 140 more shops.
➕ Off map, south ✉ 451 Long Beach Boulevard, Long Beach ☎ 310/435 8686 🚇 Metro Blue Line/Pine Avenue 🚌 60, 232

SANTA MONICA PLACE
Three storeys of boutiques, accessories, chic household goods and food court anchored by The Broadway and Robinsons-May.
➕ Off map, west ✉ Broadway at Third Street, Santa Monica ☎ 310/394 5451 🚌 20, 22, 33, SM1, 2, 8, 9

SEVENTH STREET MARKETPLACE
Relatively modest (50-unit) open-air Downtown mall boasting a brace of department stores and a gourmet food court.
➕ L7 ✉ 735 S Figueroa Street ☎ 213/955 7155 🚌 DASH A, B

SOUTH COAST PLAZA
Massive, state-of-the-art Orange County mall. European designers, US department stores, dining, children's entertainments.
➕ Off map, southeast ✉ 3333 Bristol Street, Costa Mesa ☎ 714/435 2000

UNIVERSAL CITYWALK
Eclectic gifts and souvenirs on a two-block pedestrian promenade.
➕ Off map, northwest ✉ 1000 Universal Center Drive, Universal City ☎ 818/622 4455 🚌 420, 424, 425

WESTSIDE PAVILION
Sleek, atrium-lit mall anchored by Robinsons-May and Nordstrom's. Fashions and gifts, dining and cinema.
➕ Off map, west ✉ 10800 W Pico Boulevard, West LA ☎ 310/474 6255 🚌 SM7, 8, 12, 13

Farmers' Market
Born in the 1930s Depression, at 6333 W Third Street, Midtown, when local farmers would bring their produce here in search of buyers, the market has metamorphosed into an LA institution. It's touristy, and tacky souvenirs abound, but you can still find fresh fruit and vegetables, butchers, bakers, deli counters, and great value fast food from coffee and donuts to po'boy sandwiches.

MEN'S & WOMEN'S CLOTHING

'Department Store Row'

As if Rodeo Drive were not enough to keep Beverly Hills' gold card-toting matrons occupied between lunches, LA's 'Department Store Row' lies a mere stretch limo's length away. Neiman Marcus, 9700 Wilshire Boulevard (☎ 310/550 5900), Saks Fifth Avenue, 9600 Wilshire Boulevard (☎ 310/275 4211) and Barneys New York, 9570 Wilshire Boulevard (☎ 310/276 4400), offer the full complement of fashions, furnishings, gifts and cosmetics.

AMERICAN CLASSICS
Stock up on classic US designer sportswear and casual clothing from the likes of DKNY, Calvin Klein and Converse.
➕ D3 ✉ 6825 Melrose Avenue, West Hollywood
☎ 213/954 7434 🚌 10

BIJAN USA
A more accessible version of the wildly exclusive 'open by appointment only' menswear store across the street.
➕ Off map, west ✉ Rodeo Collection, 421 N Rodeo Drive, Beverly Hills ☎ 310/273 6544
🚌 4

THE COCKPIT
Packed floor to ceiling with Americana from leather flying jackets, jeans and baseball caps to Harley Davidson bike boots, badges and collectables.
➕ Off map, west ✉ 9609 Santa Monica Boulevard, Beverly Hills ☎ 310/274 6900 🚌 4

DREAM DRESSER
Latex, leather and downright lascivious gear created with dream weavers and exotic clubbers in mind.
➕ Off map, west ✉ 8444-50 Santa Monica Boulevard, West Hollywood ☎ 213/848 3480
🚌 4

FRED HAYMAN BEVERLY HILLS
A bastion of Beverly Hills high-fashion sportswear and Academy Award night frocks.
➕ Off map, west ✉ 273 N Rodeo Drive, Beverly Hills
☎ 310/271 3000 🚌 20, 21, 22

FRED SEGAL
Legendary (and eternally hip) Melrose speciality store complex with a finger in every pie. Sportswear and designer collections, accessories, lingerie and luggage.
➕ A3 ✉ 8100 Melrose Avenue, West Hollywood
☎ 213/651 4129 🚌 10

GIORGIO BEVERLY HILLS
Veteran Rodeo Drive designer and perfumier. Ladies who lunch, charming staff and outrageous prices.
➕ Off map, west ✉ 327 N Rodeo Drive, Beverly Hills
☎ 310/274 0200 🚌 20, 21, 22

GUESS?
Fashionable and comfortable suits and casual clothing for men and women, plus great kidswear at several locations around town. Also outlet bargains in the Cooper Building (➤ 70).
➕ Off map, west ✉ Unit 3, Century City Shopping Center, West LA ☎ 310/556 0123
🚌 4

IXIZ
Modern classics for men from jeans to dress shirts via Italian knitwear and Versace. Several locations including Fred Segal (above) and Glendale Galleria (➤ 71).
➕ Off map, northeast ✉ 15 E Colorado Boulevard, Pasadena
☎ 818/793 6350 🚌 180, 181

Retro & Second-hand Clothing

AAARDVARKS' ODD ARK
Barn-like vintage clothing store. Dinner jackets from bandleader-flash to butler's tails, frocks and feather boas, accessories and wig bin. Also in Pasadena and Venice.

➕ B3 ✉ 7579 Melrose Avenue, West Hollywood ☎ 213/655 6769 🚌 10

AMERICAN RAG
Vast second-hand clothes and accessories emporium. Tuxes, grunge, ex-military great coats, '70s glam and '80s unspeakable. The works.

➕ Off map, west ✉ 150 S La Brea, Midtown ☎ 213/935 3154 🚌 14, 16, 212

AMERICAN VINTAGE
The 'worn-out-West' look – previously loved denim, Top Gun aviator jackets, bowling shirts, aloha prints, plus US collectables, vintage Zippos and Native American jewellery.

➕ C3 ✉ 645 N Martel Avenue, West Hollywood ☎ 213/653 5645 🚌 10

CASTLE COMPANY
Frock up with ladies' vintage clothing from the 1940s, '50s and '60s, in the Mission West historic district. Also costume jewellery and reproduction home crafts.

➕ Off map, northeast ✉ 1024 Mission Street, Pasadena ☎ 818/403 9595 🚌 188, 256, 483

GOTTA HAVE IT
Behind an eye-catching playing card design façade, serried ranks of wildly assorted retro wear for guys and gels.

➕ Off map, west ✉ 1516 Pacific Avenue, Venice Beach ☎ 310/392 5949 🚌 SM7

PAPER BAG PRINCESS
One-of-a-kind vintage designer dresses and accessories from the likes of Alaïa, Yves St-Laurent and Maud Frizon.

➕ Off map, west ✉ 885 Westbourne Drive, West Hollywood ☎ 310/358 1985 🚌 4

PARIS 1900
Antique lace, bows and furbelows. Original Victorian and Edwardian collector's pieces for very special occasions. Open by appointment.

➕ Off map, west ✉ 2703 Main Street, Santa Monica ☎ 310/ 396 0405 🚌 33, SM1

STAR WARES ON MAIN
Thrift-shopping with a difference: all these cast-offs have a glittering pedigree. This is the place to pick up slinky frocks and other nearly new items culled from real stars' wardrobes.

➕ Off map, west ✉ 2817 Main Street, Santa Monica ☎ 310/399 0224 🚌 33, SM1

WASTELAND
Unmissable metal and mosaic façade fronting a funky collection of velvet, vinyl and lurex delights, fluffy angora tops and leopard-print hot-pants.

➕ C3 ✉ 7428 Melrose Avenue, West Hollywood ☎ 213/653 3028 🚌 10

Rocketing back in time
If you really get into the retro thing on Melrose Avenue, Johnny Rocket's, 7507 Melrose (corner of Gardner), West Hollywood, is the ultimate 1950s-style diner where you can order up a milkshake to match your new second-hand poodle skirt or strike a suitably Jimmy Dean pose over a hamburger and monopolise the juke box. And for something completely different, don't miss the wonderfully wacky flower petal-look street lamps diagonally across the street.

ANTIQUES & ART

Mission West

South Pasadena's turn-of-the-century Mission West shopping district is a favourite haunt for antique browsing. Along pretty, tree-shaded Mission Street there are more than half-a-dozen antiques dealers including furniture and collectables at Mission Antiques, 1018 Mission; vintage clothing at Castle Company, 1024 Mission; Yoko Japanese Antiques, 1011 Mission; and Americana at Hodgson's Antiques, 1007 Mission.

ANTIQUARIUS

A great place for a browse: more than 30 shops specialising in antique jewellery, silver, art glass and collectable curios.

➕ Off map, west ✉ 8840 Beverly Boulevard, West Hollywood ☎ 310/535 7848 🚌 14

BERGAMOT STATION

This old trolley station now houses some 20 contemporary galleries dealing in an exciting range of art, sculpture, furniture, glass and photography.

➕ Off map, west ✉ 2525 Michigan Avenue, Santa Monica ☎ 310/829 5854 🚌 SM9

BROADWAY GALLERY COMPLEX

Another Santa Monica arts enclave specialising in contemporary paintings, prints and functional art with a California bias.

➕ Off map, west ✉ 2018–2114 Broadway (between 20th & Cloverfield), Santa Monica 🚌 4, SM1

GEMINI G.E.L.

Prints by top American/US-based 20th-century artists including Rauschenberg, Hockney, Jasper Johns and Richard Diebenkorn.

➕ Off map, west ✉ 8365 Melrose Avenue, West Hollywood ☎ 213/651 0513 🚌 10

LOUIS STERN FINE ARTS

Well-respected gallery specialising in Impressionist, Latin American, modern and contemporary paintings.

➕ Off map, west ✉ 9002 Melrose Avenue, West Hollywood ☎ 310/276 0147 🚌 10

MARGO LEAVIN GALLERY

An eye-catching knife sculpture skewers the façade of this cutting-edge contemporary art gallery.

➕ Off map, west ✉ 812 N Robertson Boulevard, West Hollywood ☎ 310/273 0603 🚌 4, 220

PCH ANTIQUES MALL

Ten minutes from Downtown Long Beach, 90 dealers offer a wide selection of antique glass, china, toys and furnishings.

➕ Off map, south ✉ 3500 E Pacific Coast Highway, Long Beach ☎ 310/ 494 7778

SANTA MONICA ANTIQUE MARKET

Antiques and collectables from around the world. Silver, jewellery, books, crockery, clothing and more from 150 stalls.

➕ Off map, west ✉ 1607 Lincoln Boulevard, Santa Monica ☎ 310/314 4899 🚌 SM3

SOTHEBY'S

An LA outpost of the world-famous auction house where fine and decorative works of art and antiques come under the hammer at regular sales.

➕ Off map, west ✉ 9665 Wilshire Boulevard, Beverly Hills ☎ 310/274 0340 🚌 20, 21, 22

BOOKS & GIFTS

ACRES OF BOOKS
Rambling treasure trove of second-hand tomes covering every conceivable topic.

⊞ Off map, south ✉ 240 Long Beach Boulevard, Long Beach ☎ 310/437 6980 🚇 Metro Blue Line/Long Beach Boulevard

BODHI TREE
The New Age bookstore where Shirley MacLaine got metaphysical. Philosophy, astrology, holistic healing and organic gifts.

⊞ Off map, west ✉ 8585 Melrose Avenue, West Hollywood ☎ 310/659 1733 🚌 10

BORDERS BOOKS AND MUSIC
An impressive selection of classic and contemporary literature (100,000 titles) and sounds, plus a handy in-store café.

⊞ Off map, west ✉ 1415 Third Street Promenade, Santa Monica ☎ 310/393 9290 🚌 20, 21, 22, SM1, 2

DEL MANO GALLERY
A terrific array of innovative and affordable contemporary crafts ranging from jewellery and silverware to art glass, ceramics and one-off furnishings.

⊞ Off map, northeast ✉ 33 E Colorado Boulevard, Pasadena ☎ 818/793 6648 🚌 180, 181

FEDERICO
Wonderful Native American, Mexican and Central American jewellery, pottery, textiles and antiques.

⊞ Off map, west ✉ 1522 Montana Avenue, Santa Monica ☎ 310/458 4134 🚌 SM3

GIRASOLE
Lovely gifts for the home include hand-painted Italian majolica ware, French and English small furnishings, gourmet goodies for the kitchen and scented treats for the bathroom.

⊞ Off map, northeast ✉ 38 E Colorado Boulevard, Pasadena ☎ 818/449 2500 🚌 180, 181

IMAGINARIUM
It's hard to work out who has more fun in this toy store, the adults or the children. Hands-on demonstrator models.

⊞ Off map, west ✉ Unit 320, Century City Shopping Center, 10250 Santa Monica Boulevard, West LA ☎ 310/785 0227 🚌 4, 22, 322

SMALL WORLD BOOKS & THE MYSTERY ANNEXE
Convenient beachfront emporium with everything from classics and a few foreign language books to beach holiday mysteries, sex 'n' sun 'n' shopping sagas.

⊞ Off map, west ✉ 1407 Ocean Front Walk, Venice Beach ☎ 310/399 2360 🚌 33

THE SOAP PLANT
A heaven-scent gem of a store. Groovy soaps and essential oils mingle with bath toys and typically crazy LA gift ideas.

⊞ C3 ✉ 7400 Melrose Avenue, West Hollywood ☎ 213/651 3811 🚌 10

Whale of a design district
The 'interior design capital of the Pacific Rim', West Hollywood boasts a wealth of art and antiques galleries, plus around 300 speciality design stores and showrooms centred on the west end of Melrose Avenue and San Vicente boulevards. The formerly trade-only Pacific Design Center (aka 'The Blue Whale' ➤ 55) is now open to the public with more than 200 decorator showrooms offering furniture, fabrics, floor and wall coverings, lighting and kitchen products.

MOVIE MEMORABILIA & SOUVENIRS

Ocean Front Walk

Looking for LA T-shirts, Dodgers Baseball caps, postcards and other souvenir tat? Then make a beeline for Venice Beach's open-air bazaar where the stalls are piled high with cheap LA-themed goods, $5 sunglasses, microscopic bikinis, West Coast thrash CDs, and New Age tie-dye creations.

CINEMA COLLECTORS

Mountains of memorabilia for the terminally star-struck including autographs, books, fanzines, photographs and posters.

+ E2 ⊠ 1507 Wilcox Avenue, Hollywood ☎ 213/461 6516 🚍 1

COLLECTORS' BOOKSTORE

The 'most comprehensive array of cinematic collectables on the planet' – apparently: movie stills, posters, magazines, scripts.

+ E1 ⊠ 1708 N Vine Street, Hollywood ☎ 213/467 3296 🚍 1

THE DISNEY STORE

Goofy, Donald and the Little Mermaid are joined by Lion King T-shirts, Mickey mugs and Minnie umbrellas in the great merchandise heist.

+ Off map, west ⊠ Unit 39, Century City Shopping Center, 10250 Santa Monica Boulevard, West LA ☎ 310/556 8036 🚍 4

FANTASIES COME TRUE

Disney collectables in every shape and form from famous character toys and china figurines to buttons, badges, stickers and posters.

+ B3 ⊠ 8012 Melrose Avenue, West Hollywood ☎ 213/655 2636 🚍 10

LARRY EDMUNDS' BOOK SHOP

A small but rich trawling ground for cinematic bibliophiles stocking all sorts of film and theatre-related tomes, plus posters and stills.

+ D1 ⊠ 6644 Hollywood Boulevard, Hollywood ☎ 213/463 3273 🚍 1

MGM STUDIO STORE

Your chance to dress up as an MGM/UA production crew member in official logo-strewn jackets, caps and script bags.

+ Off map, west ⊠ 2501 Colorado Avenue, Santa Monica ☎ 310/449 3300 🚍 SM9

NAME THAT TOON – ICONS OF HAPPINESS

The very best in animation art from Disney, Hanna-Barbera, Warner Brothers and new kids on the block such as *The Simpsons* and Nick Park, plus TV and movie props.

+ Off map, west ⊠ 8483 Melrose Avenue, West Hollywood ☎ 213/653 5633 🚍 10, 105

SPIKE'S JOINT WEST

Spike Lee aficionados can stock up on mementoes of their hero at this modest little store devoted to cool clothing and assorted merchandise.

+ C3 ⊠ 7263 Melrose Avenue, West Hollywood ☎ 231/932 7064 🚍 10

WARNER BROTHERS STUDIO STORE

Bugs Bunny and the Loony Tunes crew feature on all manner of souvenir paraphernalia, clothing and accessories.

+ Off map, west ⊠ 270 Santa Monica Place (Fourth & Broadway), Santa Monica ☎ 310/393 6070 🚍 4, 33

OTHER SPECIALITY SHOPS

CONDOMANIA
Descriptions seem superfluous. However, safe sex needn't be boring is the none-too-subtle message.
⊞ C3 ✉ 7306 Melrose Avenue, West Hollywood ☎ 213/933 7865 🚍 10

EVERY PICTURE TELLS A STORY
Captivating bookshop-gallery displaying original art and lithographs from children's books: Eric Carle, Tim Burton, Maurice Sendak.
⊞ B4 ✉ 7525 Beverly Boulevard, Midtown ☎ 213/932 6070 🚍 14

KALEIDO
A visual extravaganza of brilliant limited edition and one-of-a-kind kaleidoscopes and other scope-related masterpieces.
⊞ Off map, west ✉ 8840 Beverly Boulevard, West Hollywood ☎ 310/276 6844 🚍 14

LA EYEWORKS
From the town that never removes its shades even after dark, face furniture to suit every occasion.
⊞ C3 ✉ 7407 Melrose Avenue, West Hollywood ☎ 213/653 8255 🚍 10

MODERN LIVING
Cool glassblock setting for dramatic modern furnishings from the likes of Philippe Starck and comparably groovy Italians.
⊞ A3 ✉ 8125 Melrose Avenue, West Hollywood ☎ 213/655 3899 🚍 10

THE MUSEUM STORE
Fine arts, crafts, gifts, animation art and a terrific selection of classic posters by 20th-century icons.
⊞ Off map, west ✉ 2730 Main Street, Santa Monica ☎ 310/314 6700 🚍 33, SM1

THE MYSTERIOUS BOOKSHOP
A gripping source of thrilling tomes.
⊞ Off map, west ✉ 8763 Beverly Boulevard, West Hollywood ☎ 310/659 2959 🚍 14

SOOLIP PAPERIE & PRESS
Amazing stationery store lined with racks of colourful handmade papers, plus coloured inks, hip pens and desk accessories.
⊞ Off map, west ✉ 8646 Melrose Avenue, West Hollywood ☎ 310/360 0545 🚍 10

WANNA BUY A WATCH?
Vintage and contemporary timepieces from Bulova to Betty Boop, Tiffany dress watches, US military issue, plus antique diamond and art deco jewellery.
⊞ C3 ✉ 7366 Melrose Avenue, West Hollywood ☎ 213/653 0467 🚍 10

THE WOUND & WOUND TOY CO
A nostalgic array of clockwork cars, trains and trucks, plus robots, singing birthday cakes and Etch-A-Sketch keyrings.
⊞ C3 ✉ 7374 Melrose Avenue, West Hollywood ☎ 213/653 6703 🚍 10

St Elmo's Village
A hippy-funky alternative to the fashion victim chic on Melrose, this unlikely arts project in quiet suburbia welcomes visitors at the weekend. A group of old wooden bungalows with gardens full of cacti and sculpture at 4830 St Elmo Drive (off S La Brea), Midtown, fronts the mural-covered courtyard where artists offer free workshops in sculpture, painting and performance arts from 11am on Saturdays (information ☎ 213/936 3595).

CLASSICAL MUSIC & PERFORMING ARTS

Tickets

Concert and theatre tickets can be purchased direct through the venue, or through a major ticket agency such as Ticketmaster (☎ 213/381 2000), Ticket Time (☎ 310/473 1000) and Ticketron/Teletron (☎ 213/480 3232), which also supply tickets to sporting events.

Sightseeing concerts

Join the Da Camera Society (☎ 310/440 1351) for an evening of chamber music in one of several intimate and historic sites around the city. The 'Chamber Music in Historic Sites' series has visited the Biltmore Hotel, the Huntington Library and the *Queen Mary* among others.

BECKMAN AUDITORIUM
Host to the excellent Cal Tech After Dark performing arts season, which features big names in theatre, music and dance.
➕ Off map, northeast ✉ 332 S Michigan Avenue, Pasadena ☎ 818/395 3847 🚌 401

GEFFEN PLAYHOUSE
Neighbourhood theatre with a fine reputation, and intimate enough to host one-man shows.
➕ Off map, west ✉ 10886 Le Conte Avenue, Westwood ☎ 310/208 5454 🚌 20, 21, 22, SM1, 2, 3, 8, 12

HOLLYWOOD BOWL
Much-loved outdoor venue for the Los Angeles Philharmonic Orchestra's Symphony Under the Stars series (Jul–Sep) and other alfresco performances.
➕ Off map, northwest ✉ 2301 N Highland Avenue, Hollywood ☎ 213/850 2000 🚌 420

JAPAN AMERICA THEATER
Contemporary and traditional Japanese performances (Noh plays, kabuki theatre).
➕ N7 ✉ 244 S San Pedro Street, Little Tokyo ☎ 213/680 3700 🚌 DASH A

MUSIC CENTER
LA's chief performing arts complex: Dorothy Chandler Pavilion (home to the LA Philharmonic's winter season), the Ahmanson Theatre (musicals, drama and comedy) and the Mark Taper Forum (experimental productions). It is also used by the Music Center Opera and the acclaimed Joffrey Ballet.
➕ M6 ✉ 135 N Grand Avenue ☎ 213/972 7211 🚇 Civic Center 🚌 DASH A, B

ODYSSEY THEATRE
One of the city's most highly regarded avant-garde theatre companies offering a range of own-ensemble and visiting productions.
➕ Off map, west ✉ 2055 S Sepulveda Boulevard, West LA ☎ 310/477 2055 🚌 SM9

PASADENA CIVIC AUDITORIUM
Home of the esteemed Pasadena Symphony Orchestra, and a magnificent 1920s Moeller theatre organ. Also various theatre and dance events.
➕ Off map, northeast ✉ 300 E Green Street, Pasadena ☎ 818/449 7360 🚌 401

SHUBERT THEATER
Century City's saving grace if you happen to be a fan of lavish big-production musicals.
➕ Off map, west ✉ 2020 Avenue of the Stars, Century City, West LA ☎ 310/201 1555 🚌 4

UCLA CENTER FOR THE PERFORMING ARTS (WADSWORTH THEATER)
Off-campus facility offering more than 200 music and dance events a year from home-grown and visiting performers.
➕ Off map, west ✉ 10920 Wilshire Boulevard, Westwood ☎ 310/825 2101 🚌 20, 21, 22, SM2

ROCK, JAZZ & BLUES VENUES

THE BAKED POTATO
One of LA's best contemporary jazz spots, and the stuffed baked potatoes aren't bad either.
✚ Off map, northwest ✉ 3787 Cahuenga Boulevard (at Lankershim), Studio City ☎ 818/980 1615 🚌 420

B B KING'S BLUES CLUB
Restaurant and club serving Delta-style food and live blues, occasionally from the master himself. Gospel brunch on Sundays.
✚ Off map, northwest ✉ Universal City Walk, Universal City ☎ 818/622 5464 🚌 420, 424, 425, 522

HOUSE OF BLUES
This 'tin shack' on Sunset attracts massive queues and a generous sprinkling of celebs for a 'happening' combination of southern food and headline blues-rock acts.
✚ Off map, west ✉ 8430 Sunset Boulevard, West Hollywood ☎ 213/650 1451 🚌 2, 3

MCCABE'S GUITAR SHOP
Guitar store by day, R&B-rock-jazz-folk showcase with some pretty impressive names on Friday and Saturday nights. Intimate, informal, and alcohol free.
✚ Off map, west ✉ 3101 W Pico Boulevard, Santa Monica ☎ 310/828 4497 🚌 SM7

THE MINT
Long-standing small blues bar with a faithful following and a well-deserved reputation for atmosphere and great music.
✚ Off map, west ✉ 6010 W Pico Boulevard, Midtown ☎ 213/954 9630 🚌 30

THE ROXY
Small, steamy rock venue with serious street cred for its combination of major recording acts, new bands and a sound system to blow your socks off.
✚ Off map, west ✉ 9009 Sunset Boulevard, West Hollywood ☎ 310/276 2222 🚌 2, 3

SYSTEM M CAFFE GALLERY
California bar and grill that supplements good food with nightly jazz, blues and alternative music sessions.
✚ Off map, south ✉ 213A Pine Avenue, Long Beach ☎ 310/435 2525 🚇 Blue Line/Pine Avenue 🚌 60

THE VIPER ROOM
Co-owned by Johnny Depp, the Viper draws cool crowds and big names. Jam and dance nights.
✚ Off map, west ✉ 8852 Sunset Boulevard, West Hollywood ☎ 310/358 1880 🚌 2, 3

THE WHISKY
Though there is rather less of the 'Go-Go' these days, this Sunset Strip stalwart is still a haven for hard rockers.
✚ Off map, west ✉ 8901 Sunset Boulevard, West Hollywood ☎ 310/652 4202 🚌 2, 3

Classic jazz
September's LA Classic Jazz Festival is a major annual event with venues all over town. More than 200 local and international musicians set the town alight with contemporary, traditional, Dixieland, swing and ragtime sounds over a long weekend (for information ☎ 310/521 6893).

Opening times
Most music bars are open nightly from around 9PM until 2AM. Headline acts tend to go on after 11PM, when the clubs start to liven up. Clubs and music bars are often closed on Sunday and Monday nights. Call ahead to avoid disappointment.

NIGHTCLUBS

Club circuit

For the dedicated clubber with plenty of stamina and deep pockets, LA NightHawks (☎ 310/392 1500) can arrange a VIP night on the town. Limousine transport and no-hassle entry to a host of music, cabaret, dance and comedy clubs.

CHECCA RESTAURANT & NITECLUB
Continental cuisine, bar, live entertainment and dancing in civilized surroundings.
➕ C3 ✉ 7323 Santa Monica Boulevard, Hollywood ☎ 213/850 7471 🚌 4

CINEGRILL
Sleek art deco interior and an eclectic cabaret running the gamut from jazz to comedy. Deservedly popular; check it out.
➕ D1 ✉ Hollywood Roosevelt Hotel, 7000 Hollywood Boulevard, Hollywood ☎ 213/466 7000 🚌 1

COCONUT TEASZER
Loud and live rock music and dancing spread over a brace of floors with accompanying bars and a mixed crowd. '
➕ A2 ✉ 8117 Sunset Boulevard, West Hollywood ☎ 213/654 4773 🚌 2, 3

CRUSH BAR
The Continental Club's retro heart beats to the sound of 1960s to '70s Motown and soul. Great dancing; reggae and hip-hop nights.
➕ E2 ✉ 1743 N Cahuenga Boulevard, Hollywood ☎ 213/463 7685 🚌 1

THE GATE
Smart dinner-dance club with broad musical tastes from techno to hip-hop. Outdoor patios and California cuisine.
➕ Off map, west ✉ 643 N La Cienega Boulevard, West Hollywood ☎ 310/289 8808 🚌 10

MAYAN
Fashionably dressy crowd disport themselves to salsa and disco in the exotic surroundings of a former Downtown theatre.
➕ L8 ✉ 1038 S Hill Street ☎ 213/746 4287 🚌 DASH E

RITZ-CARLTON HUNTINGTON HOTEL
The Huntington's elegant grill room features live entertainment and there is dancing in the lobby lounge on Saturday nights (➤ 85).
➕ Off map, northeast ✉ 401 S Oak Knoll Avenue, Pasadena ☎ 818/568 3900

THE ROXBURY
A night out with 'the real Beverly Hills 90210 set'. Dress up and party; live music, disco, and five bars.
➕ Off map, west ✉ 8225 Sunset Boulevard, West Hollywood ☎ 213/656 1750 🚌 2, 3

STAR LOUNGE
An adjunct of the chic Abiquiu restaurant (➤ 66). DJs, live bands, outdoor dancing and salsa on Sunday nights.
➕ Off map, west ✉ 1413 Fifth Street, Santa Monica ☎ 310/236 0028 🚌 4, SM1, 7, 10

THE STRAND
Live music, dancing and dining at the hottest night spot in the South Bay.
➕ Off map, southwest ✉ 1700 S Pacific Coast Highway, Redondo Beach ☎ 310/316 1700 🚌 439

BARS

BARNEY'S BEANERY
Convival bar area with pool table and lengthy beer menu squeezed up against the Tex-Mex dining room (▶66).
🞤 Off map, west ✉ 8447 Santa Monica Boulevard, West Hollywood ☎ 213/654 2287 🚌 4

CASEY'S BAR & GRILL
Popular in the early evening with Downtown office workers. Happy hour and piano music.
🞤 M7 ✉ 613 S Grand Avenue ☎ 213/629 2353 🚇 DASH B, E

CAT 'N' FIDDLE PUB
Young, lively crowd, pleasant atmosphere and English beer on tap.
🞤 E2 ✉ 6530 Sunset Boulevard, Hollywood ☎ 213/468 3800 🚌 2, 3

CHEZ JAY
Laid-back neighbourhood beach bar with a broad clientele and a great juke box.
🞤 Off map, west ✉ 1657 Ocean Avenue, Santa Monica ☎ 310/395 1741 🚌 20, 22, 33, SM1, 10

GOTHAM HALL
Designer pool hall in the pedestrian heart of Santa Monica. Good people-watching in the bar; restaurant.
🞤 Off map, west ✉ 1431 Third Street Promenade, Santa Monica ☎ 310/394 8865 🚌 20, 22, 33, SM2, 3, 8, 9

HARVELLE'S
Neighbourhood bar-cum-terrific blues club on the Westside.
🞤 Off map, west ✉ 1432 Fourth Street, Santa Monica ☎ 310/395 1676 🚌 4, SM1, 9, 10

MOLLY MALONE'S IRISH PUB
Venerable Irish-American institution. Guinness, darts and Irish music.
🞤 Off map, west ✉ 575 S Fairfax Avenue (south of Melrose Avenue), Midtown ☎ 213/935 1577 🚌 10

MUSSO & FRANK
Hollywood's oldest and most celebrated bar and grill (▶64).
🞤 D2 ✉ 6667 Hollywood Boulevard, Hollywood ☎ 213/467 7788 🚌 1

REGENT BEVERLY WILSHIRE
Dark, clubby hotel bar with capacious leather seating and cigar-chomping clientele.
🞤 Off map, west ✉ 9500 Wilshire Boulevard, Beverly Hills ☎ 310/275 5200 🚌 21, 22

YANKEE DOODLES
Mammoth sports bar with 17,000 square feet of fun, games, billiards, pizza restaurant, arcade and sports store. Also in Santa Monica.
🞤 Off map, south ✉ 4100 E Ocean Boulevard, Long Beach ☎ 310/439 9777 🚌 LBT 121

YE OLDE KING'S HEAD
Ex-pat haunt for the local British community. Draught beer, darts, pub grub and heroic English breakfasts.
🞤 Off map, west ✉ 116 Santa Monica Boulevard, Santa Monica ☎ 310/451 1402 🚌 4, 20, 22, 33, SM1 7, 10

Liquor laws

Bars can legally open at any time between 6AM and 2AM, though most choose to open their doors around 11AM and close around midnight (later on Fridays and Saturdays). Provided they are licensed, restaurants can serve alcohol throughout their hours of business except between 2AM and 6AM. To buy or consume alcohol legally in the State of California, customers must be aged 21 or older. In a bar, nightclub or restaurant, youthful-looking patrons may well be asked to show proof of their age.

OTHER IDEAS

Catch a movie

New-release Hollywood movies often hit the screens around town months before they turn up in cinemas overseas. To catch the latest releases check what's on at the multi-screen Cineplex Odeon, Universal City (☎ 818/508 0588), or take a stroll around Westwood Village, where half-a-dozen cinemas offer everything from first-run movies to the classics, art-house and foreign-language offerings at the Nuart Theater (☎ 310/478 6379). If you dial the MovieFone service (☎ 310/777-FILM), and tap in the name of the film you want to see, it will direct you to the cinema closest to you showing that film.

BOB'S BIG BOY
Serried ranks of LA's coolest customised hot rods wheel up at this Valley diner on a Friday night. It's the Petersen (➤ 29) for real.
🚼 Off map, northwest
✉ 4211 Riverside Drive, Burbank ☎ 818/843 9334

COMEDY & MAGIC CLUB
Stand-up comedy (occasional big names) spliced with magic acts at this lively venue.
🚼 Off map, southwest
✉ 1018 Hermosa Avenue, Hermosa Beach ☎ 310/372 1193 🚌 439

COMEDY STORE
Three stages showcase funsters who are up-and-coming, have made it or are just plain HUGE at one of the city's premier clubs.
🚼 Off map, west ✉ 8433 Sunset Boulevard, West Hollywood ☎ 213/656 6225 🚌 2, 3

COUNTRY STAR
A themed restaurant for country music fans serving downhome fare, plus country star memorabilia, music and interactive video kiosks.
🚼 Off map, northwest ✉ By Universal Studios entrance, Universal City ☎ 818/762 3939 🚌 420

GRIFFITH PARK OBSERVATORY
Spectacular views of the city at night and no charge for star-gazing through the Observatory's 12in telescope (➤ 32).
🚼 Off map, northwest

✉ 2800 East Observatory Road, Griffith Park ☎ 818/901 9405 🚌 180, 181

GROUNDLINGS THEATRE
Talented improvisational comedy troupe presents short-run shows plus new talent nights.
🚼 C3 ✉ 7307 Melrose Avenue, West Hollywood ☎ 213/934 4747 🚌 10

THE IMPROV
A popular new material testing ground for big-name comics.
🚼 A2 ✉ 8162 Melrose Avenue, West Hollywood ☎ 213/651 2583 🚌 10

MOONLIGHT TANGO CAFÉ
Nostalgic 1930s/40s style Hollywood supper club locked in the Swing era with dining and dancing in the old-fashioned way.
🚼 Off map, northwest ✉ 13730 Ventura Boulevard, Sherman Oaks ☎ 818/788 2000 🚌 424, 425, 522

PASADENA POPS
Summer concerts in Descanso Gardens (➤ 57). Bring a picnic or order one with your ticket.
🚼 Off map, northeast ✉ 1418 Descanso Drive, La Canada ☎ 818/952 4400

WIZARDZ
A nightclub featuring magicians, tarot card readers, fortune tellers and dinner shows with laser displays.
🚼 Off map, northwest ✉ CityWalk, Universal City ☎ 818/506 0066 🚌 420

GYMS, SPAS & SPORTS

BALLY'S TOTAL FITNESS
A city-wide chain of health clubs with varying facilities from fully equipped weight rooms, pools and squash courts to aerobics classes and spa treatments. Call for the nearest location.
☎ 1-800/695 8111

BEVERLY HOT SPRINGS SPA
Relaxation and rejuvenation through mineral baths, massage and total body treatments.
✚ Off map, west ✉ 308 N Oxford Avenue, Beverly Hills ☎ 310/734 7000 🚌 14

BURKE WILLIAMS DAY SPA & MASSAGE CENTER
Celebrity favourite for a hedonistic range of treatments from facials and pedicures to thermal seaweed wraps.
✚ Off map, west ✉ 1460 Fourth Street, Santa Monica ☎ 310/587 3366 🚌 4, 22

GOLD'S GYM
Home of the Gold's Gym world-wide body-building empire.
✚ Off map, west ✉ 360 Hampton Drive, Venice Beach ☎ 310/392 6004 🚌 33, SM1

GRIFFITH PARK GOLF
Two 18-hole and two 9-hole courses with facilities including club rental, carts, pro-shop, dining and night-lit driving range.
✚ Off map, northwest ✉ Griffith Park Drive, Griffith Park ☎ Information and reservations, 213/485 5566 🚌 96

GRIFFITH PARK TENNIS
More than two dozen courts (available for both day- and night-use) in three locations around the park. No reservations required for Griffith Park Drive courts.
✚ Off map, northwest ✉ Griffith Park Drive and Vermont Canyon, Griffith Park ☎ Information and reservations, 213/485 5566 🚌 96

SANTA ANITA RACE TRACK
A lovely track situated in the lee of the San Gabriel Mountains. Thoroughbred horse-racing December to April, October and November. Free viewing of morning workouts and weekend tram tours.
✚ Off map, northeast ✉ 285 W Huntington Drive, Arcadia ☎ 818/574 7223 🚌 79, 187, 188, 379

TENNIS PLACE
Mid-town lighted tennis courts open until late. Pro lessons available.
✚ Off map, west ✉ 5880 W Third Street (one block west of La Brea) ☎ 213/931 1715 🚌 16, 212

WORLD GYM
Another legendary work-out facility (rivalling Gold's) for the Nautilus narcissists on Muscle Beach. Also locations in Pasadena and Burbank.
✚ Off map, west ✉ 812 Main Street, Venice Beach ☎ 310/399 9888 🚌 33, SM1

Jogging
For joggers who want to get off the city streets, LA's most attractive option is probably the 22-mile beach path running south from Santa Monica. Downtown a good place to jog is Exposition Park; there is Griffith Park in the Hollywood Hills; and, just to the west, Lake Hollywood, with a great trail around the quiet reservoir reached by car off Cahuenga Boulevard (via Dix Street).

Spectator sports
Baseball fans can catch the LA Dodgers (☎ 213/224 1448) at home at the Dodger Stadium, north of Downtown. For live basketball action, the LA Lakers (☎ 310/419 3100) play the Forum, Inglewood; while the LA Clippers (☎ 213/748 8000) are at the Sports Arena in Exposition Park.

LUXURY HOTELS

Prices

The following price bands are given on a per night minimum, based (except for hostels) on two adults sharing a standard room:

Luxury hotels – over $150

Mid-range hotels – $60 to $150

Budget hotels – up to $60.

Most hotels offer accommodation in several price ranges. If you are on a budget and the rate offered is at the top end of your limit, check to see if there is anything cheaper. If you are prepared to take a chance, many hotels are prepared to negotiate on the price if they still have vacancies later in the day.

BEVERLY HILLS HOTEL (£££)

Legendary pink palace set in 12 landscaped and palm-fringed acres. ✚ Off map, west ✉ 9641 Sunset Boulevard, Beverly Hills ☎ 310/276 2251, or US/CAN 1-800/283 8885 🍴 Two restaurants, coffee shop, poolside café 🚌 2

CHATEAU MARMONT (£££)

Famous/infamous Hollywood haunt. Film types still favour the 1927 Norman-style castle. ✚ A2 ✉ 8221 Sunset Boulevard, Hollywood ☎ 213/656 1010, or US 1-800/242 8328 🍴 Dining room with fine wine cellar (£££) 🚌 2

HOTEL BEL-AIR (£££)

LA's finest tucked away in a wooded canyon. ✚ Off map, northwest ✉ 701 Stone Canyon Road, Bel-Air ☎ 310/472 1211, or US 1-800/648 4097 🍴 Fine restaurant (£££)

HOTEL NIKKO AT BEVERLY HILLS (£££)

Sleek Japanese-inspired décor with hi-tech executive accessories. ✚ Off map, west ✉ 465 S La Cienega Boulevard, Beverly Hills ☎ 310/247 0400, or US/CAN 1-800/645 5687 🍴 Excellent restaurant (▶ 65) (£££) 🚌 20, 21, 22

NEW OTANI (£££)

Luxury hotel in Little Tokyo offering Western and Japanese accommodation. ✚ N7 ✉ 120 S Los Angeles Street ☎ 213/629 1200, or US/CAN 1-800/421 8795 🍴 Three restaurants (▶ 67) (££–£££) 🚌 DASH A

REGENT BEVERLY WILSHIRE (£££)

Sumptuous European-style grand hotel. ✚ Off map, west ✉ 9500 Wilshire Boulevard, Beverly Hills ☎ 310/275 5200, or US 1-800/427 4354 🍴 Excellent restaurant (▶ 62) (£££) 🚌 20, 21, 22

RITZ-CARLTON HUNTINGTON (£££)

Beautifully restored 1907 hotel; luxurious facilities, stunning gardens. ✚ Off map, northeast ✉ 1401 S Oak Knoll Avenue, Pasadena ☎ 818/568 3900, or US 1-800/241 3333 🍴 Famous grill room (£££)

SHERATON GRANDE (£££)

Fine Downtown hotel with oversize rooms and superb city views. ✚ M7 ✉ 333 S Figueroa Street ☎ 213/617 1133, or US/CAN 1-800/325 3535 🍴 Very good restaurant (£££), and grill (££) 🚌 DASH A

SHERATON UNIVERSAL (£££)

The best in Universal City. Good value weekend packages. ✚ Off map, northwest ✉ 333 Universal Terrace Parkway, Universal City ☎ 818/980 1212, or US 1-800/325 3535 🍴 Good restaurant (££–£££) 🚌 420, 424, 425

SHUTTERS ON THE BEACH (£££)

Lovely rooms and suites in a New England-style edifice right on the beach. ✚ Off map, west ✉ One Pico Boulevard, Santa Monica ☎ 310/458 0030, or US 1-800/334 9000 🍴 Very good restaurant (£££) 🚌 22, 33

MID-RANGE HOTELS

CONESTOGA HOTEL (££)

Old West themed hotel with good children's facilities and free shuttle to Disneyland near by.

✚ Off map, southeast ✉ 1240 S Walnut Street, Anaheim ☎ 714/535 0300, or US 1-800/824 5459 🍴 Restaurants (£–££) 🚌 460

CONTINENTAL PLAZA LAX (££)

An airport bargain with pool and more atmosphere than most.

✚ Off map, southeast ✉ 9750 Airport Boulevard, LAX ☎ 310/645 4600, or US 1-800/529 4683 🍴 Restaurant (£)

FIGUEROA HOTEL – CONVENTION CENTER (££)

Useful mid-range business hotel in central location.

✚ L8 ✉ 939 S Figueroa Street ☎ 213/627 8971, or US 1-800/421 9092 🚌 DASH C

HOLIDAY INN HOLLYWOOD (££)

A family-friendly base close to Hollywood Boulevard. Pool and helpful staff.

✚ D1 ✉ 1755 N Highland Avenue, Hollywood ☎ 213/462 7181, or US 1-800//HOLIDAY 🍴 Restaurant (££) 🚌 1

HOLLYWOOD ROOSEVELT HOTEL (££)

Refurbished Spanish Colonial-style Hollywood legend (▶ 53) with poolside cabana rooms.

✚ D1 ✉ 7000 Hollywood Boulevard, Hollywood ☎ 213/466 7000, or US 1-800/950 7667 🍴 Good restaurant (££–£££) 🚌 1

MALIBU COUNTRY INN (££)

Romantic New England-style inn.

✚ Off map, west ✉ 6506 Westward Beach Road, Malibu ☎ 310/457 9622, or US 1-800/386 6787 🍴 Breakfast included 🚌 434

LE MONTROSE SUITE HOTEL (££)

Spacious rooms and a rooftop pool terrace with amazing views.

✚ Off map, west ✉ 900 Hammond Street, West Hollywood ☎ 310/855 1115, or US 1-800/776 0666 🍴 Restaurant (££–£££) 🚌 2, 3

PASADENA HOTEL (££)

Turn-of-the-century bed-and-breakfast inn.

✚ Off map, northeast ✉ 76 N Fair Oaks Avenue, Pasadena ☎ 818/568 8172, or US 1-800/653 8886 🍴 Restaurant (££), breakfast included 🚌 483, 485

UNIVERSAL CITY HILTON & TOWERS (££)

Universal Studios packages, good family and business facilities.

✚ Off map, northwest ✉ 555 Universal Terrace Parkway, Universal City ☎ 818/506 2500, or US 1-800/HILTONS 🍴 Restaurant (£–£££) 🚌 420, 424, 425

ZANE GREY PUEBLO HOTEL (££)

The Western-writer's 1936 pueblo-style home on Catalina Island.

✚ Off map, southwest ✉ 199 Chimes Tower Road, Avalon ☎ 310/510 0966, or US 1-800/3-PUEBLO 🍴 Breakfast included

Bookings

Reservations can be made by phone, fax or mail, and should be made as early as possible. A deposit (usually by credit card) equivalent to the nightly rate will ensure your room is held until at least 6PM; if you are arriving later, inform the hotel. Credit card is the usual payment method; travellers' cheques or cash are also acceptable, but payment may have to be made in advance. The total charge will include LA's 14 per cent transient occupancy tax.

BUDGET ACCOMMODATION

Location

This is a major consideration when choosing a hotel in a sprawling city like LA, particularly if you don't drive. Most of the hotels listed are conveniently located on the main east-west transportation corridors between Downtown and the coast at Santa Monica. If you plan on staying in the city for more than a few days, consider staying in a couple of different areas (Santa Monica and Hollywood, or Beverly Hills and Pasadena, for instance).

BANANA BUNGALOW – INTERNATIONAL HOSTEL
Rooms and dorms; friendly, international atmosphere; great facilities; free airport pick-up, tours and shuttle transportation.
➕ E1 ✉ 2775 W Cahuenga Boulevard, Hollywood ☎ 213/851 1129, or US 1-800/4-HOSTEL 🍴 Restaurant (£) 🚌 420

BAYSIDE HOTEL
Great position across from the beach and one block from Main Street.
➕ Off map, west ✉ 2001 Ocean Avenue, Santa Monica ☎ 310/396 6000 🍴 Restaurants near by 🚌 4, 20, 22, 33, SM1, 7, 10

BELLE BLEU INN BY THE SEA
B&B accommodation on the beach. Ocean views; some kitchenettes.
➕ Off map, west ✉ 1670 Ocean Avenue, Santa Monica ☎ 310/393 2363 🍴 Breakfast included 🚌 4, 20, 22, 33, SM1, 7, 10

BEST WESTERN STOVALL'S INN
Large family-orientated resort hotel close to Disneyland.
➕ Off map, southeast ✉ 1110 W Katella Avenue, Anaheim ☎ 714/778 1880, or US 1-800/854 8175 🍴 Restaurants near by (£) 🚌 460

BEVONSHIRE LODGE MOTEL
Conveniently located between Farmers' Market and the Beverly Center. Pool; families welcome.
➕ Off map, west ✉ 7575 Beverly Boulevard, Midtown ☎ 213/936 6154 🍴 Restaurants near by 🚌 14

CITY CENTER MOTEL
Small and quiet Downtown hotel with pool, west of the I–110/Harbor Freeway.
➕ L7 ✉ 1135 W Seventh Street ☎ 213/628 7141 🚌 DASH B

DESERT INN & SUITES
Well-equipped rooms and good facilities close to Disneyland.
➕ Off map, southeast ✉ 1600 S Harbor Boulevard, Anaheim ☎ 714/772 5050 🍴 Restaurants near by (£), breakfast included 🚌 460

ECONOLODGE HOLLYWOOD
Handily positioned for Melrose Avenue and Hollywood sightseeing.
➕ E3 ✉ 777 N Vine Street, Hollywood ☎ 213/463 5671, or CA 1-800/628 3353, or US/CAN 1-800/446 3916 🍴 Breakfast included 🚌 10

HOLLYWOOD YMCA
Budget bet with dorms off Hollywood Boulevard.
➕ D1 ✉ 1553 N Hudson Avenue, Hollywood ☎ 213/467 4161 🚌 1

HOSTELLING INTERNATIONAL
Good-size hostel close to the Pier. Open-air courtyard, laundry, library, some private rooms.
➕ Off map, west ✉ 1436 Second Street, Santa Monica ☎ 310/393 9913 🚌 20, 22, 33, SM8

LOS ANGELES
travel facts

Arriving & Departing

Before you go

- British citizens require a valid 10-year passport to visit the US
- A visa is required if
  1) you are staying more than 90 days;
  2) your trip is not a holiday or short business trip;
  3) you have ever been refused a visa or admission to the US, or have been required to leave the US by the US Immigration and Naturalization Service; or
  4) you do not have a return or onward ticket.
  Otherwise a Visa Waiver form is supplied by the airline.
- To apply for a visa, or for more information, contact the United States Embassy Visa Information Line, London (☎ 0891–200–290).
- No vaccinations are required to enter the US unless you have come from or stopped in countries where there are epidemics.

When to go

- Sunshine and fair weather is pretty much guaranteed in Southern California from May to October. However, it is best to avoid August and September, which can be unbearably hot and sticky, and when the smog is at its worst.
- The rainiest months are November to March.

Climate

- LA basks in a mild temperate climate. Humidity ranges between 65 and 77 per cent, and the summer heat is tempered by sea breezes.
- In winter, when 70°F days can be interspersed with 50°F

nights, bring a sweater or jacket for the evening.
- During summer, the beach is sometimes fog-bound until mid-morning, but be patient and it will burn off before midday.

Arriving by air

- Los Angeles International Airport (LAX) lies 17 miles southwest of Downtown. For information call ☎ 310/646 5252.
- Car rental companies provide free shuttle bus transportation to their parking lots from the ground transportation island outside the lower level baggage claim areas.
- Well-priced door-to-door shuttle bus services (24-hours) to all areas of the city, such as SuperShuttle (☎ 1-800/554 3146), also depart from here. For others consult the telephone directory.
- The Metro Airport Service provides shuttle bus connections between all eight terminals (Shuttle A), and the remote car parking lots (Shuttle B and Shuttle C). Shuttle C also serves the terminal for bus connections to the city.
- Cabs are readily available. Depending on the traffic a fare to Downtown or Hollywood will cost $30–40.

Arriving by bus

- LA's main Greyhound/Trailways bus terminal is Downtown, at 1716 E Seventh Street. There are also terminals in Anaheim, Hollywood, Pasadena and Santa Monica.
- Information ☎ 213/629 8402 or US 1-800/231 2222.

Arriving by train

- Visitors and commuters enter the city through Union Station, 800 N Alameda Street. Located just north of Downtown, it is on the Metro Red Line and DASH shuttle bus routes.
- Information Amtrak ☎ 213/624 0171, or US 1-800/872 7245.

Customs regulations

- Duty-free allowances include 1 litre of alcoholic spirits or wine (no one under 21 may bring in alcohol), 200 cigarettes or 50 cigars (not Cuban), and up to $100-worth of gifts.
- Some medication bought over the counter abroad might be prescription-only in the US and may be confiscated. Bring a doctor's certificate for essential medication.

Departure and airport tax

- These are included in the cost of your plane ticket.

ESSENTIAL FACTS

Travel insurance

- Travel insurance is not compulsory but it is strongly recommended. Comprehensive insurance, which should include medical coverage of at least $1,000,000, for a stay of up to one week will cost around £30 per person.

Average opening hours

- Shops: Mon–Sat 9 or 10 to 5 or 6. Department stores, shopping malls and shops in tourist areas keep longer hours and may also open on Sundays.
- Banks: Mon–Fri 9–3 or 3:30; some branches open until 5 once a week; savings banks and some banks open on Saturday mornings.

National holidays

- New Year's Day (1 Jan)
- Martin Luther King Day (third Mon in Jan)
- President's Day (third Mon in Feb)
- Memorial Day (last Mon in May)
- Independence Day (4 Jul)
- Labor Day (first Mon in Sep)
- Columbus Day (second Mon in Oct)
- Veterans' Day (11 Nov)
- Thanksgiving (fourth Thu in Nov)
- Christmas Day (25 Dec)

Money matters

- The unit of currency is the US dollar (= 100 cents). Notes (bills) come in denominations of $1, $5, $10, $20, $50 and $100; coins are 50c (a half-dollar), 25c (a quarter), 10c (a dime), 5c (a nickel) and 1c (a penny).
- Nearly all banks have Automatic Teller Machines (ATMs), which accept cards registered in other countries that are linked to the Cirrus or Plus networks. Before leaving home, check which network your cards are linked to, and ensure your personal identification number (PIN) is valid in the US, where four- and six-figure PIN numbers are the norm.
- Credit cards are widely accepted.
- US dollar travellers' cheques function like cash in all but small shops; $20 and $50 denominations are the most useful. Don't bother trying to exchange these (or foreign

currency) at banks – it is more trouble than it's worth.
- An 8.25 per cent sales tax is added to marked retail prices.

Lone travellers
- Lone travellers are not unusual in Los Angeles.
- In hotels, walkable shopping districts and tourist areas (except for Venice Beach at night) travelling solo is not a problem. But all travellers, particularly lone travellers and women, should be careful and avoid unpeopled and unlit areas after dark.

Etiquette
- LA's dress code is casual. Men are rarely expected to don a jacket or tie to dine in the smartest restaurant in town.
- LA is hell for smokers. Smoking is banned in all public buildings and is illegal in restaurants; it is permitted in outdoor seating and bar areas, though it may still be frowned upon by neighbours.
- Tipping is voluntary, but 15–20 per cent is expected by waiters; 15 per cent for cab drivers; $1–2 per bag for porters; and $1–2 for valet parking.

Places of worship
- The phone book carries a comprehensive list.

Student travellers
- An International Student Identity Card (ISIC) brings reduced admission to many museums and attractions.
- Anyone aged under 21 is forbidden to buy alcohol and may be denied admission to some nightclubs.

Time differences
- Los Angeles is on Pacific Standard Time (US West Coast), three hours behind Eastern Standard Time in New York, eight hours behind the UK, nine hours behind Western Europe, 18 hours behind Sydney and two hours ahead of Hawaiian Standard Time.

Public toilets
- Public buildings are obliged to provide public toilets, which are usually but not always maintained in good condition; those in hotel lobbies, restaurants and most bars are pristine.

Electricity
- The supply is 110 volts, 60 cycles AC current.
- US small appliances use flat two-prong plugs. European appliances require an adaptor.

Tourist offices
- Los Angeles Convention & Visitors Bureau, 685 Figueroa Street, Los Angeles, CA 90017 (☎ 213/689 8822; ◐ Mon–Fri 8–5; Sat 8:30–5). Also the Visitors Information Center, Janes House, 6541 Hollywood Boulevard, Hollywood, CA 90028 (☎ 1-800/842 8467; ◐ Mon–Sat 9–5);
- Long Beach Area Convention & Visitors Bureau, One World Trade Center No 300, Long Beach, CA 90831 (☎ 310/436 3645, or US 1-800/452 7829; ◐ Mon–Fri 8:30–5);
- Pasadena Visitor Information Center, 171 S Los Robles Avenue, Pasadena, CA 91101 (☎ 818/795 9311, or US 1-800/307 7977; ◐ Mon–Fri 8–5, Sat 10–4);

- Santa Monica Convention & Visitors Bureau, 520 Broadway, Suite 250, Santa Monica, CA 90401–2428 (☎310/393 7593, Mon–Fri 9–5). Also Visitor Center, 1400 Ocean Avenue (☎310/393 7593; ◑daily 10–4).

PUBLIC TRANSPORT

- LA has a public transportation system operated by the Los Angeles County Metropolitan Transit Authority (MTA or Metro), though most Angelenos and visitors still prefer to drive.
- Buses provide the most extensive coverage of the city. Limited subway (Metro Red Line) and light rail (Metro Blue Line) services are due to be expanded rapidly in the next few years. The Metro Green Line parallels I–105 from Norwalk west to El Segundo.

Buses

- The DASH Downtown shuttle bus covers six routes around the Financial District out to Exposition Park in the south, and north to Chinatown via Union Station and El Pueblo.
- The DASH operates every 5–15 minutes, Mon–Fri 6:30AM–6:30PM; Sat 10–5, for a flat fare of 25c.
- The MTA bus services most useful to visitors are the main east–west routes from Downtown to Santa Monica, and north–south to the South Bay area.
- They operate daily 5AM–2AM, supposedly every 15 minutes, though services can be erratic. Outside these hours, reduced-service night buses ply major routes.
- The flat fare is currently $1.10; transfers cost an additional 25c. Have the correct change ready for the machine on boarding.

Metro services

- LA's proposed Metro system will revolutionise travel in the new millennium, but as yet its effects are minimal. To date the Metro Red Line subway extends only a short distance across Downtown south from Union Station.
- The Metro Blue Line between Downtown and Long Beach is up and running. The journey takes about 45 minutes, and services operate daily 5–11, with trains every 6–10 minutes in peak hours, every 15 minutes at other times. An extension to Pasadena is scheduled for 1998.

Schedule and map information

- Schedules and maps are available from the MTA, 818 W Seventh Street, Los Angeles; 515 S Flower Street (Level B), Los Angeles; 6249 Hollywood Boulevard, Hollywood (☎213/626 4455; ◑Mon–Fri varying but always 10–3:30); 5381 Wilshire Boulevard (corner of La Brea).

Taxis

- It is virtually impossible to hail a taxi in the street, except (possibly) in the Downtown financial district.
- Hotels and transport terminals are a good bet for finding a taxi, and restaurants will order a cab on request.
- Alternatively call one of the

following firms:
Independent Cab Company
(☎ 213/385 8294);
LA Taxi (☎ 213/627 7000);
United Independent Taxis
(☎ 213/653 5050).

MEDIA & COMMUNICATIONS

Telephones

- Local calls cost 20c; insert coins before dialling (no change given).
- LA has five local telephone codes, and some calls within the LA area will require more than a 20c deposit. Dial the number and a recorded operator message gives the minimum deposit.
- The area code for Downtown Los Angeles and Hollywood is 213, which should not be dialled if calling from another 213 number. If dialling outside your area code, prefix the number with '1'. For Beverly Hills, Westside, Santa Monica, Long Beach and other South Bay areas, dial area code 310; for Orange County, dial 714; for the San Fernando and San Gabriel Valleys, dial 818; for Riverside and San Bernardino, dial 909.
- Calls from hotel room phones are liable to be much more expensive than those made on a public phone.
- Many businesses have toll-free numbers, prefixed 800. Callers must first dial '1' (ie '1–800').

Post offices

- Minimum charges for sending a postcard or airmail letter (weighing up to an ounce) overseas are currently 50c and $1 respectively. Stamps are available from post offices.
- Find the nearest post office by checking the phone book or asking at your hotel. Most open Mon–Fri 7–5; Sat 7–1.

Newspapers and magazines

- LA's only major English-language daily newspaper is the *Los Angeles Times*, which covers international and local news.
- The free *LA Weekly* is another good source of information, and the free tourist-orientated magazines distributed to hotels offer dozens of discount coupons for sightseeing attractions and restaurants.

Radio and television

- LA's airwaves hum with everything from jazz to 'shock jocks' to Spanish language and religious programmes. As a rule, the best talk radio is on the AM stations; the best music on FM.
- In addition to all the national network channels, many hotels have cable TV, pay-to-view movies and the Welcome Channel, a visitor information broadcasting service.

EMERGENCIES

Sensible precautions

- LA has an appalling reputation as a high-crime city largely, but not entirely, based on a handful of areas which few visitors will ever see. These include the notorious South-Central district, and East LA, which should be avoided altogether.
- Venice Beach is also an undesirable neighbourhood after dark.

- The easiest way to wind up in the wrong neighbourhood is to take a wrong exit off the freeway. Always plan your journey in advance, and try to check which exit you want by consulting the car rental agency, hotel staff, or call your destination.
- To foil potential pickpockets in busy or touristy areas such as the airport, do not carry easily snatched bags and cameras.
- Only carry as much cash as you require.
- Most hotels provide safe facilities for a nominal charge, where you can leave passports and other valuables.
- Replacing a stolen passport begins with a visit or phone call to your country's nearest consular office.
- Report any lost or stolen items to the nearest police precinct (see Lost Property) if you plan to make an insurance claim.

Lost property

- Los Angeles International Airport: each airline has its own lost-and-found telephone number. Airport police: ☎ 310/417 0440.
- MTA (Metrobuses and Metrolink): ☎ 213/937 8920.
- Otherwise call the relevant police precinct; addresses and phone numbers are listed in the phone book.

Medical treatment

- Many hotels can arrange for referrals to a local doctor or dentist. Alternatively, look under 'Physicians and Surgeons' or 'Dentists' in the *Yellow Pages*.
- Most city hospitals accept emergency cases. Those with well-equipped 24-hour casualty departments include: Cedars-Sinai Medical Center ✉ 8700 Beverly Boulevard, West Hollywood ☎ 310/855 5000; and Good Samaritan Hospital ✉ 1225 Wilshire Boulevard, Los Angeles ☎ 213/977 2121.

Medicines

- Pharmacies are plentiful in Los Angeles; look in the *Yellow Pages*.
- Although many familiar drugs will be available (probably under unfamiliar names), if you are using medication regularly it is preferable to bring an adequate supply (see Customs Regulations).
- If you intend to buy prescription drugs in the US, bring a note from your doctor.

Emergency telephone numbers

- Fire, police or ambulance: ✉ 911 (no money required);
- Travelers' Aid: ☎ 213/468 2500.

Consulates

- Australia ✉ Century Plaza Towers, 19th Floor ☎ 310/229 4800.
- Denmark ✉ 10877 Wilshire Boulevard ☎ 310/443 2090.
- Germany ✉ 6222 Wilshire Boulevard ☎ 213/930 2703.
- Netherlands ✉ 11766 Wilshire Boulevard, ☎ 310/268 1598.
- New Zealand ✉ 12400 Wilshire Boulevard ☎ 310/207 1605.
- Sweden ✉ 10880 Wilshire Boulevard ☎ 310/441 3763.
- UK ✉ 11766 Wilshire Boulevard ☎ 310/477 3322.

INDEX

A

Abalone Cove 60
accommodation 84–6
airport 88
airport and departure tax 89
Angel's Flight 54
aqueduct 12
Armand Hammer Museum of Art 26
Automatic Teller Machines (ATMs) 89
Autry Museum of Western Heritage 33
Avalon 21
Avila Adobe 17, 41

B

banks 89
Banning Residence Museum 50
bars 81
beaches 60
Beit Hashoah 51
Belmont Shores 42
Beverly Hills 27
Biltmore Hotel 56
boat trips 19
Bradbury Building 39
Broadway Historic Theater District 52
bus tours 19
buses 88, 91

C

Cabrillo Aquarium 59
cafés and coffee shops 68
California Heritage Museum 24
California Plaza 54
Capitol Records Tower 54
Carol & Barry Kaye Museum of Miniatures 58
Catalina Island 20–1
Century City 54, 71
Chiat-Day Inc Advertising Building 54
children's attractions 58
children, dining with 64
Chinatown 17
cinemas 82
City Hall 54
City of Los Angeles Film & Video Permit Office 52
classical music 78
climate 9, 88
Coca-Cola Bottling Factory 54–5
comedy venues 82

concert and theatre tickets 78
consulates 93
credit cards 89
crime and personal safety 90, 92–3
currency 89
customs regulations 89

D

Descanso Gardens 57
Disneyland 48
Doizaki Gallery 40
Downtown 6
dress code 90

E

El Pueblo de Los Angeles 41
electricity 90
emergencies 92–3
Ennis-Brown House 56
entertainment 78–83
etiquette 90
excursions 20–1
Exposition Park Rose Garden 57

F

Farmers' Market 63, 71
festivals and events 22
First Interstate World Center 54
Flying, Museum of 58
food and drink 62–9
Forest Lawn Memorial Park 7, 52
Franklin D Murphy Sculpture Garden 59
Frederick's of Hollywood Lingerie Museum 30, 52
free attractions 59
freeways 6

G

Gamble House 44
gardens and green spaces 57
Garment District 70
George C Page Museum of La Brea Discoveries 50
Getty Center 25
Getty Museum, J Paul 20
Grand Central Market 16, 38, 63
Grave Line tours 53
Greystone Park 57
Griffith D W 12
Griffith Park 32
Griffith Park Observatory 32, 82
gyms and spas 83

H

helicopter tours 19
Hermosa Beach 60
Higashi Hongwanji Buddhist Temple 40
historic buildings 56
history 9, 10–12
Hollyhock House 34
Hollywood Boulevard 30
Hollywood Guinness World of Records Museum 30, 58
Hollywood History, Museum of 53
Hollywood Memorial Park Cemetery 52
Hollywood Roosevelt Hotel 30, 53, 85
Hollywood sign 55
Hollywood Studio Museum 53
Hollywood Wax Museum 30
hotels 84–6
House of the Holocaust 51
Huntington, The 46

I

itineraries 14–15

J

James Irvine Garden 40
Japanese-American Cultural and Community Center 40
Japanese-American National Museum 50
Japanese Village Plaza 40

K

Knott's Berry Farm 58

L

La Brea tar pits 50
landmarks 54–5
Leo Carrillo State Beach 60
limousine tours 19
liquor laws 81
literary LA 7
Little Tokyo 40
lone travellers 90
Long Beach 42
Long Beach Museum of Art 42
Los Angeles Central Library 56
Los Angeles County Museum of Art (LACMA) 28

CityPack
Los Angeles

Written by   Emma Stanford
Edited, designed and produced by
[AA] Publishing

Maps   © The Automobile Association 1997
Fold-out map © RV Reise- und Verkehrsverlag Munich · Stuttgart
© Cartography: GeoData

Distributed in the United Kingdom by AA Publishing, Norfolk House, Priestley Road,
Basingstoke, Hampshire, RG24 9NY.

The contents of this publication are believed correct at the time of printing. Nevertheless, the
publishers cannot be held responsible for any errors or omissions or for changes in the details
given in this guide or for the consequences of any reliance on the information provided by the
same. Assessments of attractions, hotels, restaurants and so forth are based upon the author's
own personal experience and, therefore, descriptions given in this guide necessarily contain an
element of subjective opinion which may not reflect the publishers' opinion or dictate a
reader's own experiences on another occasion.
We have tried to ensure accuracy in this guide, but things do change and we would be grateful
if readers would advise us of any inaccuracies they may encounter.

A CIP catalogue record for this book is available from the British Library.

ISBN 0 7495 1426 4

Published by AA Publishing (a trading name of Automobile Association Developments
Limited, whose registered office is Norfolk House, Priestley Road, Basingstoke, Hampshire
RG24 9NY. Registered number 1878835).

Colour separation by Daylight Colour Art Pte Ltd, Singapore
Printed and bound by Dai Nippon Printing Co (Hong Kong) Ltd.

Acknowledgements
The Automobile Associaiton would like to thank the following photographers, libraries
and associations for their assistance in the preparation of this book.
The Armand Hammer Foundation 26a; Gene Autry Western Heritage Museum 33b;
Rob Holmes 55b; The Hulton Getty Picture Collection Ltd 12; The Huntington Library
46; J Paul Getty Museum 25a, 25b; Los Angeles County Museum of Art 28; Photos
courtesy of Los Angeles Convention & Visitors Bureau/ C 1995 5b, 6, 7, 13a, 30b; Museum
of Neon Art 51(Lili Lakich); Norton Simon Art Foundation 45b; Petersen Auto-motive
Museum 29a, 29b; Rancho Los Alamitos 43; © 1996 The Walt Disney Company 48.
The remaining pictures are held in the Association's own library (AA PHOTO
LIBRARY) and were taken by PHIL WOOD with the exception of pages 19, 36, 49b, 60
which were taken by ROB HOLMES.
Cover photographs
Tony Stone Images

JOINT SERIES EDITOR *Josephine Perry*
COPY EDITOR *Moira Johnston*
VERIFIER *Catherine Chambers* INDEXER: *Marie Lorimer*

Titles in the CityPack series
• Atlanta • Bangkok • Berlin • Chicago • Hong Kong • London • Los Angeles •
• Madrid • Montréal • Moscow • Munich • New York • Paris • Prague • Rome •
• San Francisco • Singapore • Sydney • Tokyo • Vienna • Washington •